President Trump And The New World Order

The Ramtha Trump Prophecy

by Michael Knight

Copyright

ISBN:
978-0-692-94853-8

Table of Contents

Acknowledgments

My sincere thanks and appreciation to JZ Knight. As Ramtha's exclusive channel since 1977 she has enabled tens of thousands of people from around the world to learn remarkable truths that have been denied the common man, and woman, for thousands of years.

I would also like to thank Christine Barrett, Andre Cyr, Chuck Bradshaw, Cindy Skakun, and JoAnn Phelps for their voluntary assistance and attention to detail in proofreading this book. And John Stribling for the unique cover art.

Disclaimers

Apart from the direct quotations by Ramtha, the views expressed herein are those of the people concerned and do not necessarily represent or reflect the views of JZK Inc., JZ Knight, or Ramtha's School of Enlightenment.

Likewise, North Star Publishing Inc. does not necessarily concur with observations and statements by sources referenced in this book, nor can the accuracy of such sources be guaranteed.

Nothing contained herein should be construed as advice of any kind. North Star Publishing Inc. shall not be held liable for the consequences of any decisions or choices made by any reader of this work.

All the direct Ramtha quotes in this publication are used with permission from JZ Knight and JZK, Inc. No part of these direct quotes may be reproduced or transmitted in any form or by any means, electronic or mechanical, including photocopying, recording, or by any information storage and retrieval system, without the written permission of JZK, Inc. All rights reserved.

Ramtha® is a registered trademark of JZ Knight and is used with permission.

JZ Knight and JZK, Inc., do not necessarily endorse or support any of the views or commentaries, in part or in whole, expressed in this publication by its authors and editors.

For more information about Ramtha's teachings contact: Ramtha's School of Enlightenment, a division of JZK, Inc., P.O. Box 1210, Yelm, WA 98597, USA. www.ramtha.com

About This Book.

This book is about the Rothschild Dynasty, the Deep State and the New World Order agenda, all of which are aspects of the pyramid of power that President Trump is up against.

But as outrageous as it may seem, especially if you are a skeptic, as the author once was, President Trump has friends in high places - one of them being Ramtha the Enlightened One.

Ramtha's prophecy may also seem outrageous - but there is visual proof that what he predicted about Donald Trump's plane being escorted by UFOs actually did happen.

For centuries the elite have inhabited the top of the pyramid of power. They have plotted and planned and established control of everything below, from politicians to nations, and the rest of us, the ordinary people of this world - the people the dynasty considers usable and expendable.

This book explains how they did it, and how President Trump may be the one to finally blow the lid off that pyramid.

In essence, that is the surprising prophecy about President Trump around which this book is based. In fact, you can see that 3-minute prophecy for yourself at www.northstarnewsletter.com.

Although he is an enigma to many, Ramtha the Enlightened One has been presenting teachings and prophecies for the past 40 years through his exclusive channel, JZ Knight.

Among those many dissertations he has revealed the history of the small group of elite individuals who have, in almost complete secrecy, and over a period of several hundred years, plotted to control the world.

This book takes those truths of history, as given by Ramtha and confirmed through many other sources, and presents the current situation as it now exists with the election of President Donald Trump - a man that Ramtha describes as "fearless," - which he needs to be, considering he is up against a faction which has ruthlessly manipulated, and sometimes assassinated, presidents in the past.

"Graymen" is Ramtha's term for a group of families (he mentions the Rothschilds specifically) who have manipulated entire nations - right down to the common man and woman - with the intention of bringing about their New World Order.

That, as you will discover, is the mother of all conspiracies.

We look at the way bankers have imposed a system on the world - and on all people - through the establishment of central banks, thanks to the assistance of corrupt or ignorant politicians.

We also investigate how the elite have conspired to create false flag events, plotted wars well in advance, and profited to the tune of trillions of dollars while the average person struggles to make ends meet, and much of the world survives on as little as $2 a day.

Relevant quotes from Ramtha - unique to this book alone - either predict or explain events in such a way that you may be either shocked, or enlightened - or both.

Either way, instead of being misinformed by the mainstream media, you will be well informed about the truth, and the future.

About The Author

Michael Knight is an award-winning journalist who began his career in New Zealand in 1960.

He was twice awarded the Hoben Prize for Journalism, was a winner in a national short story contest, and has co-authored two books, *"Building With Logs in New Zealand,"* and *"Playboys of the South Pacific,"* the seafaring life of John Glennie who would later survive 119 days in his upturned trimaran.

Michael Knight has worked internationally in all media.

He spent three years in Australia, initially as assistant public relations manager for Hamersley Iron Pty Ltd in Western Australia, then as a newsreader at TVW7/6IX in Perth.

His assignments in various capacities as a reporter, cameraman, photo-journalist and documentary director, editor and script writer have taken him to Australia, the UK, Canada and the United States.

He had his own public relations company in New Zealand, and was Editor of the quarterly *"Future Times"* magazine for the New Zealand Futures Trust, while also working on contract as a reporter/director for the long-running TV One weekly *"Country Calendar"* program.

His experience in covering national elections and seeing first-hand how politicians can "hide their true intent behind nice smiles and honeyed words," as well as discovering that there was indeed an "unseen hand" pulling their strings from behind the scenes started an investigation that has been ongoing since the 1970s.

As an investigative reporter but also for personal reasons he traveled to Yelm, Washington, in 1988, "sensing a possible expose of yet another fraudulent spiritual movement," this one involving the channel JZ Knight (no relation) and the entity Ramtha.

After two years of careful scrutiny and attending follow-up events at Ramtha's School of Enlightenment he chose to move to the United States in 1990, "which speaks for itself. You have to see for yourself instead of making up your mind based on other people's opinions."

His only response to those who question the validity of the school is - "It is a school - not a religion - and I chose to come here and pay for my education, like any student does at any college or university. I had my doubts initially, but my personal motto as a reporter looking for truth was always very simple. *Don't trust hearsay, or other people's opinions, especially the media. If in doubt - find out - for yourself.* "

Who Is Ramtha?

"Ramtha lived as a human being 35,000 years ago on the ancient continent of Lemuria. The Lemurian culture was highly spiritual. Due to dramatic Earth changes, many Lemurians migrated from what is now the U.S. Pacific Northwest through Mexico into the Atlantic basin (then Atlantis). As a young boy, Ramtha was a part of that pilgrimage. Atlantis was an advanced, technologically oriented civilization. The Lemurians were thought to be soulless by the Atlanteans (or 'Atlatians' as Ramtha calls them) and subjected to the worst kinds of abuse. At 14, Ramtha became a conqueror who freed his people from Atlantean tyranny. He became the greatest of all warriors, for his ignorance and hatred were overwhelming and he feared nothing.

"Many people from all races joined Ramtha's crusade. Over the course of 63 years, he conquered two-thirds of the then-known world. Traces of this march can be found in the remnants of ancient traditions. The great warrior was also known as Rama of the Hindu religion, the first God of the people of India. Late in his march, Ramtha barely survived a brutal assassination attempt. During his seven-year recovery, he contemplated the mysteries of nature, the life force, and what his people from Lemuria called the Unknown God. From that long study, he learned to leave his body and ultimately to take his body with him. This was his greatest enlightenment. Finally, he ascended in front of his people, promising to return."

In His Own Words

"I am Ramtha, a sovereign entity, who lived a long time ago upon this plane called Earth, or Terra. In that life I did not die; I ascended, for I learned to harness the power of my mind and to take my body with me into an unseen dimension of life. In doing so, I realized an existence of unlimited freedom, unlimited joy, unlimited life. Others who lived here after me have also ascended.

"I am now part of an unseen brotherhood who loves mankind greatly. We are your brothers who hear your prayers and your meditations and observe your movements to and fro. We are those who lived here as man and experienced the despair, the sorrow, and the joy that all of you have known. Yet we learned to master and transcend the limitations of the human experience to realize a grander state of being.

"I have come to tell you that you are very important and precious to us because the life that flows through you and the thought that is coming to every one of you — however you entertain it — are the intelligence and life force that you have termed God. It is this essence that connects all of us, not only to those upon your plane but to those in untold universes which you have not yet the eyes to see.

"I am here to remind you of a heritage which most of you forgot long, long ago. I have come to give you a loftier perspective from which you may reason and understand that you are indeed divine and immortal entities who have always been loved and supported by the essence called God. I am here to help you realize that only you through your sublime intelligence have created every reality in your life, and with that same power you have the option to create and experience any reality you desire." [Excerpted with permission from *"The White Book,"* p 21, published by JZK, Inc.]

Who Is JZ Knight?

JZ Knight is the unique channel of Ramtha and author of the best-selling autobiography, *A State of Mind, My Story*. Historians and religious experts who have studied her life's work call JZ Knight the Great American Channel and recognize her as one of the most charismatic and compelling spiritual leaders of the modern age. JZ Knight and Ramtha have captivated and inspired audiences worldwide for four decades, bridging ancient wisdom and the power of consciousness together with the latest discoveries in science.

JZ Knight is the president of JZK, Inc., and Ramtha's School of Enlightenment (www.ramtha.com), a unique academy located in the foothills of Mount Rainier in Washington State. The school was established in the 1980s and has hosted over 30,000 students from the United States and 70 foreign countries. JZ Knight is the channel through which Ramtha delivers his message. Ramtha is an ascended Master Teacher who learned in his lifetime the unlimited potential of our minds for creating reality and the extraordinary in our lives. His powerful message of hope for humanity has already changed countless lives — none more powerfully and dramatically than JZ's own life.

After 40 years of leaving her body, traveling through the tunnel of light and returning again in a fashion similar to those reported by people who have near-death experiences, JZ Knight turned her genius to reproducing one of those out-of-body environments here on Earth. She collaborated with Dr. Matthew Martinez, D.C., and together they developed a prototype called the Blu Room — "on Earth as it is in heaven." The Blu Room creates an atmosphere that insulates the experiencer from the daily environment. The participant is provided with a mind/body/Spirit and consciousness-lifting environment that can augment one's state of creative focus and the body's natural healing abilities. Since June 2015, Blu Room Enterprises, LLC (www.bluroom.com) has licensed 40 Blu Rooms worldwide.

JZ Knight is also the owner of JZ Rose (www.jz-rose.com), a treasure chest that offers vintage-style gifts and collectibles, home furnishings, fine antiques, and everything beautiful. Her personal love for fine art, timeless antiques, and nostalgic romanticism inspired her to create a store where she could share the things she loved with other people.

Some of the many humanitarian charities JZ Knight has sponsored through the JZ Knight Humanities Foundation have been the empowerment of women, world peace, and education scholarships for young adults. Since 1988, she has contributed nearly two million dollars to graduating high school seniors so they could pursue their educational goals. JZ Knight's Mercy Blu Program provides access to Blu Room treatments for individuals with debilitating health conditions at no charge.

> "I refuse to let anything blind me to possibility."
> — JZ Knight

The Tyrants - An Introduction

As background for those who may not be familiar with Ramtha and his teachings on the world and its future, it was a series of teachings by him in 1987, and events held by Ramtha's School of Enlightenment since then, that became the book *"Last Waltz of the Tyrants, The Prophecy Revisited,"* within which Ramtha coined the term "graymen."

The "graymen," says Ramtha, are today's Rothschild dynasty.

He revealed that as many as 12 or more families have worked very hard behind the scenes for hundreds of years to further their goal of complete control of the world, their desire being what is known these days as a "New World Order."

They are understood to have hundreds, if not thousands, of adherents in many places of influence. This includes Royalty, governments, corporations, the pharmaceutical industry, the military/industrial complex, religion, banks, the corporate-controlled media, the various branches of the military, many of the world's intelligence agencies, universities, and an unknown number of black budget projects.

Between them, these so-called elite families have planned many wars, financed all sides, and introduced privately owned and operated Central Banks, such as the US Federal Reserve, to all but a handful of countries around the world.

By doing so, they control not only a country's economy, but also its politicians and governments, not to mention their ownership or control of all the major corporations as well.

So ruthless are they that they resort to blackmail, bribery and murder, either to recruit people of interest, corrupt those who can help them politically, or kill those who threaten to unmask them.

They have been responsible for many assassinations, including political opponents in various countries as well as prime ministers and United States presidents.

President Lincoln was one of them, but so too was President John Kennedy. President Kennedy knew what he was up against, spoke about it, and was killed as a result.

President Kennedy's assassination in Dallas, Texas, in 1963 followed a speech he made in 1961 in which he said:- *"For we are opposed around the world by a monolithic and ruthless conspiracy that relies on covert means for expanding its sphere of influence - on infiltration instead of invasion, on subversion instead of elections, on intimidation instead of free choice, on guerrillas by night instead of armies by day."*

When Did It Start?

It all started with the Rothschild dynasty that Ramtha refers to in the book *"Last Waltz of the Tyrants."*

They and their adherents, which these days we might refer to as The Deep State, or neocons, have also been the driving force behind "free trade" agreements, the establishment of the United Nations, various trading blocs, and the European Union, all of them sold to the public as ways to improve living standards, increase employment, and provide for the safety of the populace.

All of which have been lies.

Aside from literally planning wars and financing despots such as Hitler, they have been responsible for crashing economies and creating world-wide destitution (depressions) and poverty.

Part of their plan has been to get rid of the rising Middle Class because their financial independence - as opposed to the dependency of the lower classes, the poor and impoverished, could become a real threat to their goals.

Financially independent people, sovereign people, are much harder to control than those who are dependent on others for income, shelter, utilities, home and food.

The graymen's *modus operandi* (their fundamental way of operating) has been to create a problem, watch the reaction, and offer a solution. And it has worked extremely well for a long time, because those solutions inevitably involve more laws, more loss of freedoms for the average person, and therefore tighter control for the controllers.

The graymen are masters at creating and turning chaos to their advantage, for they continue to thrive only when there is separation, animosity and wars between people, nations and empires.

After the Brexit vote in the UK - the vote to leave the European Union - it also seemed obvious that there would be more chaos throughout the EU as other nations began to demand a similar referendum, and some are certainly thinking about it.

Add to that the tremendous problems caused by the influx of hundreds of thousands of refugees from those created wars in the Middle East, and it seems possible that they'd like to generate so much chaos across Europe that before long there will be a clamoring for a world government, a New World Order.

If that is what they're after, and it certainly is, that is not the future as portrayed by Ramtha in *"Last Waltz of the Tyrants."*

The graymen might still imagine they have control of the game, in part because their plan to introduce "the card" was so successful.

It has proven to be an incredibly effective means of gaining control over hundreds of millions of people.

Ramtha was one of the very few, perhaps the only one outside the cabal, who could see what the introduction of credit and debit cards would do for the future.

The Card And Consequences

Since the 1980s when the idea of a plastic card was being sold to
the public, credit and debit cards have become, for most people,
the basic method of making transactions.

The cards are so convenient virtually no-one would imagine they
have come at the cost of giving up choice and freedom. They cost
the issuing banks virtually nothing to make, and they reap millions
in fees, outrageous fees in most cases, from those who don't pay on
time.

In 2015, the average American household owed $7,281 on their
cards; looking only at indebted households, the average
outstanding balance was over $15,000. And it keeps going up.

Unfortunately, it also means that what people think of as "credit" is
in reality debt. It also means that those who provide the loan (the
"credit") literally control those of us who have taken on the debt,
which is precisely what Ramtha warned about - though he said at
the time that taking the card was a matter of choice.

Millions of us have since learned that some choices have serious
consequences.

Money Control - Mind Control

In a nutshell, the Rothschild dynasty built its fortune by financing
governments, corrupting politicians, loaning money at interest, and
promoting wars.

They and their fellow travelers are said to be the architects of what
is currently called The New World Order. It is not yet fully in
place, but it has been a long-term goal, fortunately (one would
hope) with receding chances of completion.

Nevertheless, gathering intelligence, as the Rothschilds did and still do, was central to their plans for world control.

In the days of the horse and buggy and sailing ships they had a courier service throughout Europe that could cross borders unquestioned, their red leather saddlebags or satchels signifying that they were carrying documents of great import to kings and governments, and to the Rothschild brothers who operated banks in different countries.

At the time of Napoleon's loss of the Battle of Waterloo that fast courier service enabled Nathan Rothschild to receive intelligence ahead of the British government, and thereby manipulate the London stock exchange.

He was on the floor of the stock exchange when a courier arrived and handed him some papers. Rothschild made a show of opening them immediately. Then he adopted a forlorn look and signaled to his waiting agents on the floor to begin selling stock.

Seeing this happen, other agents began dropping stock like hot potatoes, and prices went through the floor, allowing other Rothschild agents to get busy buying at bargain prices.

Then, when the truth that Wellington had beaten Napoleon at Waterloo became known, prices skyrocketed (some say either 13 or 15%) and Nathan Rothschild made a fortune.

Nathan Rothschild is quoted as having said:- *"I care not what puppet is placed upon the throne of England to rule the empire on which the sun never sets. The man who controls Britain's money supply controls the British Empire, and I control the British money supply."*

Through their bank in London, and the establishment of banks throughout the Empire, the graymen progressively spread their tentacles world-wide, including eventually the establishment of the Federal Reserve Bank in the United States.

The Rothschild family got its start well before the Battle of Waterloo in 1815, but that is something that has been kept well hidden by the mainstream media - most of which is owned by the Globalists themselves.

To quote Ramtha once again, *"it is from this family that you will begin to see what is crumbling in the equality of human beings all over the world. The plan continued in his hands, his family, and those who were chosen to work with him, and they began to control Europa."* - Ramtha, *"Last Waltz of the Tyrants,"* p 26.

Little by little they have had legislation enacted that over a period of decades has progressively turned once free men and women into tax-paying slaves - though it has been done so stealthily that the average person would still insist that they are free. So ruthless are they that they planned various wars, and have had assassins kill those who out of conscience would not go along with their plans.

The point is, the control of money and the gathering of intelligence, especially about military, political, commercial and financial matters, enables those who gather it to profit in many ways, not only materially and financially, but far more importantly, in terms of increasing power and control. That, in turn, has been used to further the New World Order goal of the "graymen."

Hopefully, this next quote from Ramtha will provide some consolation.

"I do not wish you to think that this whole mess is hopeless. It isn't. It smells but it is not hopeless, for enlightenment is to come out of ignorance and out of the darkness." - Ramtha, *"Last Waltz Of The Tyrants,"* p 63.

Money Control - World Control

Any country which has a central bank, such as a Federal (not) Reserve, and which borrows money, must eventually dance to the tune of the money lenders.

The Rothschild dynasty and its adherents have been extremely wise, in that they know how to appeal to the egos of politicians around the world; and through such institutions as the World Bank and the International Monetary Fund (IMF) they can dictate future policy - always in order to drive nations further into debt, and to reap ever more profits for themselves.

Nations that borrow money are in exactly the same position, although on a bigger scale, as any of us who have accepted a credit card.

Those of us who have them have indeed given our power and our independence away because everything we use them for is instantly logged in the belly of the beast, a super computer system, and that leaves us wide open to even greater control if/when these cards are replaced by the next iteration. And they always are.

Until recently it was feared that the next step in population control would be an injected chip that would hold even more personal data, and be required for any purchase at all - and which could be deactivated instantly should we prove undesirable to our Orwellian overlords.

Although such chips have certainly been used in trials, and a version is happily implanted in their animals by pet owners who fear the loss of their poodle, the public outcry and resistance was such that the overlords, in a stroke of genius, came up with a much better plan, at least from their point of view.

They introduced a new card, with a gold chip emblazoned on it. Psychologically, this equates to wealth, and acceptance of that card has been widespread, especially since the banks hold the whip hand. They now send out the new card with a covering letter extolling all its virtues and advantages.

But at the same time, they tell you your current card will stop working on a certain date (not necessarily the actual expiry date written on it) and you have until then to activate your new gold-chipped plastic fantastic.

Those new cards can contain far more personal information about you than you will ever know for sure, plus they too can be switched off or rendered unusable at any time by those who control the data base.

If this seems a little far-fetched, consider these realities for a moment. Your card has a direct connection to your bank account. When you use it, anywhere, the computer it is connected to checks your bank balance and either approves or declines the transaction.

Take this a step further. Consider the way we all shop on line. We visit a site and peruse what's available or what's of interest. Maybe we open an account or establish a wish list. Suddenly we find a list across the bottom of the page telling us we have "recently viewed" a variety of products.

If this is possible for the millions of online shopping sites, it is surely just as possible for all the personal information we enter into our various transactions to be collected, collated, and stored in "the beast" - some vast computer somewhere that has assigned a number to us, keeps a record of everything we do on line, knows how much we have in the bank, selectively monitors what sites we visit (commercial or not) and builds a dossier or data base that can be accessed by those who favor a New World Order.

Taking this another step further, from that information they can build algorithms and fancy ways of targeting us with advertisements akin to our interests - or simply shut down our access to our bank account and leave us just about as useless and homeless as the most destitute person on skid row.

It's interesting, in fact quite disturbing to note also that there is currently an almost world-wide push to get rid of cash as a medium of exchange - once again with the rubric or propaganda that this will help cripple the drug trade, stop terrorism, and keep us all safe.

None of those promises has ever been fulfilled.

Banks can still be hacked, identities stolen, and the drug trade is under the control of the Illuminati anyway. Why else would opium poppy production be at record levels in Afghanistan after 16 years of US occupation when the trade had almost been eliminated under the Taliban?

However, as Ramtha said in the 1980s:-

"But when the one world government and the idealism of the graymen go forward full thrust and the debit card is issued upon the collapse of world monetary systems, your Constitution and Bill of Rights will be restructured for the new world order and what you know this day in your time will fall into antiquity. That is the plan, but it doesn't necessarily mean it will happen." - Ramtha, *"Last Waltz of the Tyrants,"* p 113.

Expanding Awareness

What's In A Name?

While the graymen have had hundreds of years to make progress with their secret agenda, they do not seem to have counted on the effect of the Internet.

In just a few decades people around the world have opted in to what you could best describe as a global but artificial brain.

Within that world wide web, so much in fact like the web of neurons in one's own brain, there is a mountain of information available, including a great deal about the graymen themselves.

It's a subject that has yet to go completely viral, but nevertheless we have seen numerous demonstrations in recent years at various locations where the elite meet to discuss their next moves.

Meetings such as the Bilderbergers, or the World Trade Organization come to m ind, as does the most recent G20 meeting at which demonstrators were said to have caused millions of dollars in damage, and in overhead costs related to security measures.

That expanding awareness of the duplicity and corruption of those in power resulted in the UK referendum and the vote to exit the European Union. Since then there have been calls for similar referendums in many other EU countries, while in the United States there have been demonstrations over fraud in the Democratic Party primaries.

Hillary Clinton's loss in the presidential race should also be seen as a rejection of elitist policies, although the msm (the mainstream, propaganda machine) would have you believe that Russia somehow got President Trump elected.

In America, and elsewhere, we can see an expanding collective consciousness that is demanding change on many levels.

Not only are these people demanding political changes, there is a growing demand for alternatives to fossil fuels, for respect for the world's forests and Earth's many resources that are currently being brought to the threshold of total depletion, and in many cases extinction.

There is a demand for free energy as demonstrated by Nikola Tesla; a demand for the release of patents on many devices that have been hidden away from the public; a demand that inventive geniuses be able to function without fear of being "disappeared".

Unfortunately this has happened to many who have challenged the status quo in the hope of bringing forward engines that run on water, or cures for cancer and so much more.

It is said that Tesla was killed by the military for access to his secrets, and they have since developed engines and look-alike UFOs that operate on an anti-gravity system.

All this must surely be anathema to the Deep State, also known as the Neocons, the Cabal, or the dynasty, started as it was several hundred years ago by a single individual with the unassuming name of Bauer.

In the beginning of the Rothschild family's long-range plan to control the world, way back in the mid-1700s, the first Rothschild was not a Rothschild to start with.

The German family name was actually Bauer, which translates from German to English as "farmer." Then try translating "farmer" back to German, and you come up with not only "farmer," but also "peasant," "yokel," and "peasant farmer."

If those were the prevailing attitudes toward the family of Bauer, even though they were money lenders, it's no wonder that, with their ambitions toward gaining acceptance in the upper echelons of society, they would change their name.

Even today, "peasant" and "yokel" and "peasant farmer" are seen by most people as derogatory terms. The name "Rothschild," (which translates as Red Shield) surely sounds a little better than Bauer with its connotations of "yokel" and "peasant farmer."

But as a general rule, farmers are not stupid people.

They have their capital, which is their breeding stock, which eat grass that costs the farmer nothing.

The breeding stock mate and give birth to both replacement animals and others to sell in order to cover costs and make a profit.

Should the carrying capacity of the farm at any time reach a point that it is overstocked, the farmer simply sends excess animals to the slaughter house - problem solved.

Now transfer that analogy to the world of capitalism.

In the case of this particular Bauer family whose ancestors probably were farmers, Mayer Amschel Bauer's father was in fact a money lender and the proprietor of a counting house. You might say he was a money farmer - a man who could use money to breed more money, cover costs and make a profit.

So good did the Rothschilds become at that, that they were eventually financing all the royal houses of Europe - and dining at the king's table no doubt, which they do to this day.

Their Golden Rule

It is said that a true alchemist can take a base element, such as lead or perhaps sand, and through a secret process requiring daily focus and long patience, turn it into gold.

Conversely, and it's a shock to realize this, the Rothschilds have proven time and again over almost 300 years, that you can do the opposite. They have taken gold and turned it into false promises, paper, then plastic, and ultimately into a digital blip on a computer.

This means you really can create money out of thin air, and, better still, you still have the original gold in your pocket, and you can buy even more with the paper and plastic and digital keystrokes that have now taken the place of gold itself.

Really, it's not so much an alchemical process in the true sense of the word. It is more a manipulative process, but in some respects it is pure social alchemy - turning your average base human into a virtual "pot of gold" from birth.

Perhaps Anton Bauer started off with a quill pen and some parchment, diligently working by candlelight as he played with numbers, dreaming perhaps of a future in which it could all be done by some beast of a machine.

Building The Pyramid

This Is How It Works

For thousands of years humanity has been involved in trading goods and services.

In some cases a bale of beaver pelts might be traded for one or two buffalo hides, while in other cultures, gold and silver and jewels would be used to purchase whatever a buyer might desire from a vendor.

Then somewhere in the middle, there developed the money man - the guy who had enough gold on hand to dream up the idea of lending it to merchants with an interest rate tacked on so he could get his loan back in full, plus an extra percentage, without having to do any manual labor at all.

Let's imagine we're back in those times. The merchants are fine with this arrangement, because it seems to mean they can borrow money beyond what they already have, then buy whatever goods they wish to trade in, sell those goods at a profit (they hope) and make enough to repay the loan, plus the interest, and still have enough profit left over to make it all worthwhile. By the look of it, it's a win-win for everyone.

Now for the sake of simplicity, let's say the money lender in Germany (the banker) has 10 customers who have each deposited 10 bars of gold. One of his sons is now a money lender in England, and he also has 10 customers and 10 bars of gold.

The German banker comes up with an idea. He tells one of his customers "we have a new really safe way to keep your gold safe. So safe and secure that you won't have to risk being robbed as you travel and do business."

"How's that?" says the German merchant who wants to buy goods in England and bring them back to sell in Germany.

"What we can do is give you a paper note which will promise you that you can check it in to our sister bank in London and get a bar of gold in return so you can buy your goods over there, bring them back, sell them, and everyone is happy."

The merchant thinks this is a great idea. He will be in no danger of being robbed on his way to England, where he will pick up a gold bar and go about his business. He accepts.

In London he goes to the bank to exchange the note for the promised gold (it's called a promissory note) where the banker greets him with a handshake and a smile and says "yes, we have the gold, but for safety's sake, your safety of course, and to help the public and your fellow merchants, we have a new system in place. You'll love it. It is so convenient and it will make it much easier for you to do business."

The merchant is skeptical but he listens. After all, he has no choice.

"What we've introduced," says the banker, "is a line of paper notes in many denominations. We've distributed them all over England, so you can trade with anyone, anywhere, without having to carry gold with you. It remains safe here in our bank. But you can always bring in those notes and exchange them for the equivalent in gold that we have safely in the vault."

The merchant says this seems like a good idea and goes along with it.

Meanwhile the banks in Germany and other countries are doing the same thing, and before long, because they promise the holder that they can be redeemed for gold, paper notes become so popular and convenient that transactions are soon done predominantly in paper, with only a small percentage of people going to the bank to get the solid gold itself.

In another stroke of twisted greed, the bankers then take advantage of that, and print more promissory notes than there is gold available to redeem them.

They have accurately deduced that it's a fair bet that not all the merchants will run to the bank at the same time (that's called a run on the bank, and with that subterfuge the system continues to work in the banks' favor.

Eventually, there is far more paper money floating around the world than there is gold in the vault to back it, but by now everyone thinks paper money is money.

Like them or not, those bankers and money lenders are smart. They are also extremely greedy, and that attitude of greed has been around much longer than the Rothschilds and the graymen.

The Death Pledge

Moneylenders have always insisted that borrowers put up assets as collateral so that if the borrower defaults for any reason, they get to own those assets. This is called a mortgage - the root of the word mortgage being "mort" - which stems from the Latin, morte, or death.

English lawyers came up with the concept long ago. Working on behalf of the money lenders they drew up binding documents that anyone wanting a loan, such as for buying a house, would be required to agree to.

They had to sign a "death pledge," which would end (or die) when the loan was paid off, or in the event of the borrower's inability to continue paying off the loan, perhaps because of death, the bank could take over the mortgaged assets for closure of the loan, (hence the word "foreclosure").

Nothing much has changed in the centuries that bankers have been loaning money to those prepared to sign a death pledge. Today's reality is very much like that, but with yet another twist.

Those with 30-year mortgages can be paying 30 per cent or more of their income to meet their payments. In many cases this now requires both partners to work full time to avoid losing the roof over their heads and the land under their feet.

For centuries, the elite have been fine-tuning their system, to the point that the average person has no idea at all how the modern system works - or how it keeps us all functioning as virtual slaves almost from the day we are born - the day on which we get our Social Security Number; a number that will eventually reside in the belly of the beast.

Exposing The Pyramid

How It *Really* Works

Many years ago I did a stint as economics correspondent for Television One in New Zealand.

On a day off I was driving somewhere and picked up a hitch-hiker.

It turned out that he was from Switzerland, where he had just graduated with a PhD in Economics.

We chatted for a while about the state of the world, but things got really quiet when I popped my Big Question.

"Who owns the money?"

To me, it seemed like a very reasonable question. Every other commodity I could think of had a source and an original owner. This would be followed by other owners as the goods changed hands, but ownership was built into the whole process.

Therefore, asking "who owns the money?" was meant to find out who the original owners might be.

The question was never answered definitively. All I got was "Money is like air. Everyone has access to it. Nobody owns it."

Looking back on that brief discussion, it seems that the PhD guy did give me what to him was a reasonable answer. It was also extremely accurate in one way at least. I didn't say so, but money, as far as I could tell, was indeed made out of thin air. Imagine that. Gold comes out of the ground. Money comes out of thin air.

All these years later, thanks to three books *"The Unseen Hand,"* *"The Tower of Basel,"* and Ramtha's *"Last Waltz of the Tyrants,"* I have realized the question itself was slightly flawed. Instead of asking "who owns the money?" I should have asked "who *controls* the money?"

Who controls the money in this modern day and age? Ramtha explained that in *Last Waltz of the Tyrants* in which he again mentions the Rothschilds.

"The name of this man in the 1800s was Rothschild. Remember that, because it is from this family that you will begin to see what is crumbling in the equality of human beings all over the world. The plan continued in his hands, his family, and those who were chosen to work with him, and they began to control Europa. They created dictators out of common people, feeding them through their altered ego. They created assassinations. They created blame, outbreaks, and dissension all for power and money. The money brought them the power, because every man had his price and every kingdom certainly had its price." - Ramtha, *Last Waltz Of The Tyrants*, pp 26/27.

Although he is not named in that quote, Hitler was one of the dictators financed by banks controlled by the Rothschilds and their associates, as was Napoleon.

Napoleon is credited with saying *"When a government is dependent upon bankers for money, they and not the leaders of the government control the situation, since the hand that gives is above the hand that takes... Money has no motherland; financiers are without patriotism and without decency; their sole object is gain."* - Napoleon Bonaparte, Emperor of France, 1815.

Ramtha goes on to say:- *"Since the time of Napoleon every war has been manipulated, set up, and financed by the graymen and their families. If the inkling of war didn't exist, they created it at any cost. Remember, these families had no allegiance to any country, had no allegiance to any of its laws, and had no allegiance to any religious belief. They were on their own, which allowed them to do this quite nicely.*

"In 1857, throughout Europe, other places around the world, and the beginning of this country, the Rothschild dynasty had placed those individuals in important decision-making positions who were beholden to or in allegiance with this family. In 1857 there was a meeting in London. There they plotted all the wars that would occur in Europa and this country to as far back as World War II, the last war plotted." - Ramtha, *"Last Waltz of the Tyrants,"* p 27.

That means that the elite, the bankers, plotted to start World War I. It must also mean that, despite what we've been told by our official historians, Germany was set up, and then, having lost that conflict, it was required to pay billions of dollars in reparations to the countries it had fought.

This was an extremely difficult if not impossible situation for Germany, but another perfect opportunity for the bankers and their tame politicians.

The Bank of International Settlements

The cartel of families and bankers decided to set up a new bank to handle the reparations issue.

To achieve this, they came up with a new plan in 1926. Four years later, with the willing cooperation of partners in many countries, they established the Bank of International Settlements (BIS) in the Netherlands in 1930.

We know this from the BIS website itself, which says that on *"20 Jan 1930 The Final Act of the Second Hague Conference is adopted by heads of state and government representatives. This includes the agreement between the central banks of Belgium, France, Germany, Italy, Japan and the United Kingdom and a financial institution representing the United States to set up the Bank for International Settlements."*

Who or what was the "financial institution representing the United States?" They don't say. Which makes one ask, how is it that the representative of a financial institution can sign on to something on behalf of an entire nation?

Within a year the BIS was headquartered at Basel in Switzerland, yet it is independent of Switzerland, not subject to any Swiss laws, operates tax free, and enjoys something akin to the status of an embassy, which in turn offers diplomatic immunity to its people.

In short, the BIS is above the law, and its people can't be charged with any crimes, no matter what they do in the way of money laundering and so forth.

The BIS was quickly recognized worldwide as the head of the global financial system.

The most important point here, is that this was, and is, a privately owned and operated bank. From Day One it has taken its orders from the "elite," orders which would become the rules of conduct for privately owned banks, central banks in particular, throughout the world - or at least the vast majority of it.

Rules of conduct mean different things to different people. During World War II the Nazis and their allies stole huge amounts of gold from the thousands of Jews they exterminated and the countries they invaded.

Looted Gold

From Adam LeBor's book, *"Tower of Basel,"* which is an in-depth look at the Bank of International Settlements, we learn that *"Under Thomas McKittrick, the bank's American president from 1940-1946, the BIS was open for business throughout the Second World War. The BIS accepted looted Nazi gold, conducted foreign exchange deals for the Reichsbank, and was used by both the Allies and the Axis powers as a secret contact point to keep the channels of international finance open."*

Much of this purloined gold found its way into the vaults of the Bank of International Settlements, no questions asked, at least, perhaps not until 1944 and the Bretton Woods conference.

None of the above is mentioned on the BIS website itself. In fact, the one entry that has anything to do with the reparations background simply says, without any explanation:- *"9 Jun 1969 A BIS Extraordinary General Meeting amends the Statutes to delete all references to the 1930 Young Plan."* (The Young Plan had to do with reparations settlements).

Keeping in mind LeBor's statement that the BIS *"accepted looted Nazi gold,"* we find another entry on the BIS site that suggests that the BIS had served its purpose and was no longer required. *"Jul 1944 The United Nations Conference in Bretton Woods agrees to the creation of the International Monetary Fund (IMF) and the World Bank; it also adopts Resolution V calling for the liquidation of the BIS at 'the earliest possible moment'."*

That did not happen, and it just may be a coincidence, though probably not, because on *"13 May 1948 (came the) Washington Agreement: the BIS reimburses looted gold it had inadvertently received from the German Reichsbank during the war to the Allied Tripartite Commission. The Bretton Woods resolution calling for the liquidation of the BIS is put aside."*

That meeting, which smells of a negotiated compromise, would ensure that the Bank of International Settlements would continue to sit at the top of the world banking pyramid, immediately below it being the International Monetary Fund, the World Bank, and then the multitude of Central Banks, such as the Federal Reserve in the United States.

The Pyramid - At The Top

Along with the BIS, the IMF and the World Bank, these privately owned central banks sit at the top of the world's financial pyramid, and they also enjoy all sorts of immunities.

In essence, they are untouchable. Which probably explains why they can be bailed out to the tune of billions of dollars when they (pretend to) get into trouble, and why none of their executives ever get more than a slap on the hand despite engaging in truly nefarious schemes.

The truth of it is that taxpayers, the general public, Joe Six-pack and Rosy the Riveter, you and me, we are all at the bottom of the pyramid.

We and our parents and grandparents, our children and grandchildren, are the ones who are sent to manufactured wars where we die.

For what? For what we believe to be a righteous cause, never realizing we have been sent to the killing fields by a small group of psychopaths who are motivated only by greed and their lust for power.

Because they control the amount of money that is available at every level of the pyramid, they control nation after nation, which includes the millions of us at the bottom of the pyramid. And they are ruthless.

In times past, when Europe was ruled by the Catholic church, lending money with interest was forbidden. In fact, it was punishable by death. Not so today. The world we live in is awash in debt from the highest to the lowest levels - except for the elite.

Under the guise of "helping" a country, the IMF and the World Bank carefully negotiate a deal and a debt that they know the country will never be able to repay.

It is actually a sophisticated form of extortion, because through their connections with major corporations they can then require that they be "paid in kind," which simply means allowing the resources of that indebted country to be taken over by corporations which, in essence, engage in looting those assets. At a huge profit, of course.

Corrupt politicians and ignorant finance ministers go along with these schemes, sometimes having been set up and blackmailed, or willingly bribed. Or else they are both naive and ignorant and really believe they are helping their fellow man, not realizing they are only helping the few at the top.

The Pyramid - At The Bottom

To bring this idea of how debt actually enriches the rich down from Wall Street to Main Street, to those of us at the bottom of the pyramid, we should take a close look at the interest rates we pay on what we purchase - a house for instance.

First up, both credit, and interest, are debts.

We sign a contract, which creates a loan, artificially known as a credit, but it also creates a debt, which is the interest on the loan.

Let's say for the sake of simplicity that we get a loan (a credit) of $100,000. The interest rate is 5%.

Not only do we have to repay the loan on fixed terms at a certain amount every every month every year, we also have to find the additional money to pay the 5% interest, which usually comes out of our salary or income.

In other words, that interest rate depletes your income, so you are effectively that much poorer every month and every year for the full term of the loan.

As far as the loan itself is concerned, did they give you $100,000 in real cash and have you deposit it in your account?

Not at all.

They simply created $100,000 with a few keystrokes on a computer.

No doubt they took a lien on your new house as well - allowing them to repossess it in the event you should default on the loan.

Therefore, those keystrokes not only created "money" out of thin air, the contract also ensured that the bank could take your property - a real asset - should you ever be forced to default.

In other words, while you might think you personally own the property, you will not own it at all, until the loan, plus the interest, is fully paid off.

Money For Nothing

As for the interest, that is said to be a usage cost - the cost of "using" the bank's money (which it just made out of nothing).

Say your $100,000 loan is for 20 years at 5% per year. You have to find $5000 every year, just to cover the interest. In 10 years, you would have paid out $50,000; in 20 years, it will be $100,000.

Your $100,000 house has , in reality, cost you $200,000.

You worked 20 years to pay it all off, and the bank worked maybe a couple of hours - or less - to make $100,000 in interest, after creating the $100,000 loan out of nothing.

How do they do that, and get away with it? Because, like it or not, this system that would make a Ponzi scheme look like a safe bet, is all legal. It's called fractional reserve banking.

Before we discuss that, we have another quote from Ramtha about the graymen.

"By 1920 the graymen had grown to twelve families. They were the individuals who owned the international banks and literally Switzerland itself. They were the ones who incorporated that gold no longer be convenient to carry around. They were the ones who created paper money. They created the bank of London. They owned the bank of London. They created a major Federal Reserve in every major country where they printed money according to their desire and their plans for power. Finally, after a few unfortunate incidents in this country, the Federal Reserve Act was passed where the Federal Reserve could now print monies in this country, paper monies, which were no longer necessarily backed by gold. In other words, it was worthless. They created an economy on a worthless piece of paper because of their manipulative control." - Ramtha, *"Last Waltz Of The Tyrants,"* p 31.

Fractional Reserve Banking

Economists tell us that fractional reserve banking is the system in most countries around the world. It allows banks to accept deposits which are immediately recognized as the bank's reserves.

On the books, they are also known as liabilities, since depositors might wish to withdraw their money at some future time.

Nevertheless, while in the bank, those deposits are legally the property of the bank and not the depositor.

Let's say you deposit $1000 in the bank. The bank might say it now has a liability of $1000. But it can also say it has $1000 of reserves.

The reason it is called "fractional reserve banking" is that the bank only needs to hold reserves equal to a fraction of what it creates in the way of loans. Therefore, if for example the bank need only hold 10% in reserve, while you have deposited $1000, the bank can now legally loan or invest $900 of your deposit elsewhere - and of course they'll be charging interest on it as well.

Banks lend out or invest 90% of what people deposit, gambling that not everyone will want their money back at the same time. If they did, it would be a "run on the bank," and they would be ruptured - "bankruptered."

Although it is a privately owned bank, the Federal Reserve in the US furthers the charade that it is a government entity with its website titled www.federalreserve.gov where you can find much more information about reserve requirements.

Personal experience with banks, house and vehicle loans and credit and debit cards over the past 50 years, along with some serious research into the machinations of the New World Order cabal has led to the inescapable conclusion that it's not money, but the money lenders, which are, so to speak, the root of all evil. But they couldn't do what they have done without the assistance of greedy or power-hungry politicians.

The President Who Ruined America

For many of us, the endless bleeding of our income by way of taxes at so many levels is indeed an evil we could do without.

Why is it that we are taxed in the first place?

The answer goes back to the establishment of the Federal Reserve in 1913, the borrowing of money by the Federal Government and the need to pay the interest on those loans.

It's the same scenario as getting a loan to buy a house - you have to find the interest payments out of your own income. But what if, being the Federal Government, you did not have a substantial additional income other than tariffs on incoming goods, as was the case back then? Where would you get the money to pay back your loans and the interest on your debts?

Where would they get that from - the country's citizens of course. Hence, the introduction of income taxes. However, which came first? The loan? Or the income tax?

The Federal Reserve Act was passed on December 23 1913, and unless one does some additional research, one is likely to think that income taxes were introduced thereafter in order to cover the interest on whatever loans the government negotiated.

In fact, the Revenue Act of 1913 came first, being signed into law by President Woodrow Wilson on October 3 1913, thus imposing a federal income tax while lowering tariffs from 40% to 25%.

That no doubt was a great benefit to the English companies, and those from other countries, which traded with America.

Wilson's Way

Virtually on Christmas Eve, 1913, America's Federal Reserve Act was signed into law by President Woodrow Wilson.

Wilson would one day say that ... *"The government, which was designed for the people, has got into the hands of the bosses and their employers, the special interests. An invisible empire has been set up above the forms of democracy..."*

And ... *"Some of the biggest men in the United States, in the field of commerce and manufacture, are afraid of somebody, are afraid of something. They know that there is a power somewhere so organized, so subtle, so watchful, so interlocked, so complete, so pervasive that they had better not speak above their breath when they speak in condemnation of it..."*

And ... *"I am a most unhappy man. I have unwittingly ruined my country. A great industrial nation is controlled by its system of credit. Our system of credit is concentrated. The growth of the nation, therefore, and all our activities are in the hands of a few men.*

"We have come to be one of the worst ruled, one of the most completely controlled and dominated Governments in the civilized world, no longer a Government by free opinion, no longer a Government by conviction and the vote of the majority, but a Government by the opinion and duress of a small group of dominant men."

Like many presidents before and since, Wilson obviously became aware that there was indeed a force behind the throne, behind the system, behind the government that literally worked to control the world through the power of money.

Did he know this before he was elected?

He certainly knew that his opponent, sitting President William Howard Taft, had promised to veto any central bank legislation. Taft was adamantly against the Federal Reserve Act, which had been in the works well before Wilson became president, but Wilson's win as a Democratic candidate resulted in its passage within just a few months of his taking office.

By doing that, he gave control of America's finances, and its future, to the bankers - the Rothschilds and their fellow travelers. By introducing the income tax, which would supposedly pay off any interest rates on loans taken out by his and future governments, he also indebted all future generations to those bankers.

A hundred years later, that debt is $20 trillion.

President Wilson also ensured that America would enter World War I - one of the many wars that had been planned by the cabal - and he did so by sacrificing over a thousand lives.

Ramtha - WWI

"It took a lot to get this country into the First World War because no one wanted to get into it. The graymen owned most of the media. They owned all the papers and said what to print and what not to print, because it was also important to have control over what the people read. They went on and on in a media campaign for this war about the patriotism of this country, and those who did not see that the banner of liberty always flows freely were considered traitors. There was a very hot political campaign that went on in this country to ensure that that war occurred. Do you remember the incident that got you into that little pickle? Yes, sinking your ship. Did you know that passenger ships leaving the shores of this continent were already carrying contraband and supplies? Your country got into it. How brave were all your sons and some of your daughters who died in that war for liberty to free Europe from the menace of Germany. What a lark. It wasn't that at all." - Ramtha, *"Last Waltz Of The Tyrants,"* pp 29/30.

Why would the graymen have planned such a holocaust? Because their goal has always been world control. Regardless of the cost in human lives.

They have been masters of the art of subterfuge, utilizing false flag events on many occasions to manipulate public opinion, which has been easy to do because of their ownership and control of most if not all the major media, not only in the US, but throughout Europe and much of the world as well.

Without that media control, America may never have entered World War I,or World War II, or Korea and Vietnam and Afghanistan and Iraq and now Syria as well.

The media played a critical role for the graymen when they set up the sinking of the Lusitania, just as today's mainstream media has been diligent in convincing the public that war was essential after the tragedy of 9/11.

Take CNN for instance. Established as the Cable News Network it is currently embroiled in a war of words with President Trump, who frequently accuses them of being "fake news."

This is precisely what the graymen want - fake news or derogatory news about President Trump - because the election of this president has really upset their New World Order agenda.

Others who have noted this propensity for bad journalism and empty talking heads have called CNN the "Clinton News Network," or the "Criminal News Network" - which leads to a further off-the-cuff suggestion; how about calling it the "Cabal News Network"?

It would be unkind to say all the journalists in all the media are in a sense puppets or, worse yet, ventriloquists' dummies, but some of them most certainly are.

Paying as much as $150,000 for a degree in journalism does not a journalist make. Rather, it produces individuals who have learned a formula, such as "if it bleeds it leads," and if it doesn't, at least imply that it did, or it could have, or it might, or it will. And don't ever forget the ratings because your job depends on advertising income.

Journalism is also a cover for agents of the various intelligence services, while ownership of the media gives the oligarchs the best of all worlds. Lots of money, but also the ability to deliberately manipulate and even polarize audience perception.

Remember, the cabal has controlled the media for a very long time, always to their advantage, as was the case during President Wilson's tenure and the deliberate sinking of the Lusitania.

Lusitania - False Flag

The cabal has not only orchestrated numerous wars, with the assistance of a compliant media that refuses to ask the tough questions, it has set them up with false flag events, just one example being the sinking of the British Cunard passenger liner, the Lusitania, on May 7 1915.

Britain was already at war with Germany, but America was neutral - with President Woodrow Wilson in office - the man who signed the Federal Reserve Act into law, and who would now assist the cabal in its determination to embroil the United States in World War I.

Germany was using U-boats to harass and sink the ships of Britain and its allies, but studiously avoided hitting those of neutral countries, such as America.

In secret, it was determined by those at the highest levels of government in Britain and the US that if enough American lives were lost at sea, American citizens would respond with outrage and quickly join the conflict.

The plot was hatched. It was decided to use the British ship, the Lusitania, and a false manifest suggesting the ship was only carrying butter, cheese and furs, along with about 1900 passengers.

Instead, she was loaded with six million bullets, 50 tons of shells and other explosive materials (gun cotton impregnated with pyroxiline, manufactured by Du Pont, that would blow up when exposed to salt water), then sail her into harm's way off the Irish coast, where U-boats were known to be operating. On this one voyage, she was denied the escort of destroyers that had seen her safely through troubled waters on previous occasions.

The plot worked. The Lusitania was hit by a torpedo, and the secondary explosion sent the vessel down within 18 minutes. Nearly 1200 people, including 128 Americans, died in a matter of minutes, although there were 764 survivors.

The orchestrated cover-up blamed the captain for the tragedy, while Woodrow Wilson and his colleagues mounted a huge propaganda campaign which eventually saw the US enter the conflict - a war that cost 65 million lives in a matter of four years.

The cabal considered itself to be well on the way to achieving its goal of global governance. Wilson was their handy spokesperson in establishing the League of Nations after that war - but as we know, it was not as successful as expected, eventually being replaced by what is now the United Nations edifice.

Wilson actually suffered a defeat at home in this regard. While he had signed the Treaty of Versailles that established the peace process and the League of Nations, he had no such authority under the US Constitution. The government of the day refused to join, seeing full well that it would do away with America's hard-won sovereignty.

War Is Peace

As hard to swallow as it might be, the subterfuge of pretending to do things for the benefit of humanity (and the "preservation of Democracy" which was Wilson's war cry) has been used to this day to con people into seeing others as the enemy, and so we engage in endless war on the pretext of establishing peace.

In reality, those wars have been about tightening the control of the Illuminati, plundering available resources, and making corporations billions from supplying the weapons of war, and then more billions for other corporations that are awarded reconstruction contracts.

Aside from reducing the world population by 65 million in World War I alone, the graymen benefited as well from other aspects of their plan. Again under Wilson, the United States passed the Espionage Act of 1917 (and amendments in 1918) that made it an offense to "obstruct the sale of bonds ... or the making of loans to ... the United States." Punishment? A mere $10,000 fine (in 1917 money) and/or 20 years in prison. PLUS - the same penalty for anyone who might "utter, print, write or publish any disloyal, profane, scurrilous or abusive language about the form of government of the United States."

Considering Wilson's election as a Democrat, Americans were being primed to accept Democracy as their form of government, rather than the Republic system on which the nation was founded. What they did not understand (to this day) is that a democracy inevitably becomes a two-party system, and if you are rich enough to support and donate to your favored candidates in both parties, regardless of who wins you have control of the country, while the people believe their vote actually counted for something.

Next in this short list of major benefits for the Illuminati - money. Money. Money. For them, money control equates to the power to control.

Before World War I America had a debt of $1 billion - perhaps a manageable one at the time now that the income tax act had been established; but by the end of that war, the US was $25 billion in debt - in just three short years.

Can we see the bankers of the time laughing all the way to the bank - and ever since?

As their associations and power have grown over recent centuries, they have stitched together what amounts to a 10,000-piece jigsaw puzzle; a puzzle that the vast majority of people are neither willing to look at, nor desire to solve.

Ramtha - What Do They Want?

"What is it they want? Absolute power, and absolute power is to take their idealism of a One World Order where the whole world, with invisible borders, will be ruled sort of like social fascism. The elite will rule you all, and the selling point behind this is that there will be no more wars. With a one world government everyone is equal, except the elite, and they will progress humanity without revolution, without war, and without pestilence to a further aristocracy. In other words, Middle America and the humans who live in far-off places you don't know about are indeed to become slaves, and many of them deserve it because they have created the vacuum for it to occur. They want to be told what to do. They want someone to make decisions for them. They don't want to be bothered with it. They want someone to tell them what is going to go on the next day because they do not want to be bothered. That is One World Order." - Ramtha, *"Last Waltz of the Tyrants,"* pp 50/51.

If we looked at that statement objectively, we'd have to conclude that it is true, at least of the vast majority of people in this world.

Surely that is why the Illuminati, the cabal, the Rothschilds and Rockefellers and rotten politicians have been so successful for so long in manipulating public opinion; molding it through both subtle and extreme methods, such as false flag incidents that serve to drive nations to war.

Those who question and analyze and criticize are certainly in the minority, and much of what they have to say, if it is covered at all by the mainstream media, is buried in the back pages or the late night news - except when such critics become such a threat to those in power that they suddenly wake up dead.

Without dwelling further on the subject of false flags, we can simply add that Pearl Harbor was a false flag that got America into World War II; an incident in the Gulf of Tonkin led to the loss of 50,000 American lives in Vietnam, and the false flag of 9/11, which murdered at least 3000 innocent people as the Twin Towers came down in a controlled demolition, has been a multi-multi-billion-dollar success for the cabal, the military/industrial/political complex, and all those at the top of the pyramid.

The Business Model

For the Illuminati, everything is a business model. Everything they plan and instigate must yield a profit, be it in money, power or additional control of the world.

That is why their private banks, loans, debt and inflation serve them so well on so many levels.

There are also things called Bonds. You'd think with a name like that that it means something like *"my word is my bond, and if you buy these bonds, by my word I will repay you with interest - and in gold coin to boot."*

You'd be wrong. Very wrong.

Under the guise of helping to pay the costs associated with America's entry into World War One, $16 billion worth of so-called Liberty Bonds were issued in 1917 and 1918. They were to mature in the 1920s, but could be rolled into a later issue with better terms. Those terms included the principal and interest being payable in gold coin "of the present standard of value," which it was claimed would prevent an investor being harmed by inflation.

Came time for redemption in 1934, just a year after President Roosevelt had taken America off the gold standard, and the investors were ripped off by the Treasury Department, which reneged on the undertaking to pay in gold coin - a loss to investors in today's terms of about $225 billion.

No doubt the government was held to blame for their loss, but then, and even today, most people believe the Treasury Department is an independent bureaucracy, when in fact it works hand in glove with the privately owned Federal Reserve,. and even draws its staff from the major Wall Street banks.

As their associations and power have grown over recent centuries, the bankers and their cohorts have stitched together what amounts to a 10,000-piece jigsaw puzzle; a puzzle that the vast majority of people are neither willing to look at, nor desire to solve.

Inflation Is Theft

Because governments inevitably overspend and go over budget, just like most people do, they are constantly applying for more loans or rolling over the ones they have which in turn incurs more interest in terms of debt that they can never repay.

Whether you are an individual or a government, in order to cover that debt you have to find money in addition to what you are repaying on the loan.

How do you do that?

You can work harder and longer, make more money, and pay the interest (debt).

Or if you are a government, you can raise taxes, which in turn depletes the real income of your debt-laden citizens; or you can allow the banker surrogates (corporations) to harvest your country's resources, such as copper, gold, coal, iron ore, and so on.

You can even, under the guise of cutting back on wasteful government expenditure, thereby "improving efficiency," privatize such things as the prison service, which in reality benefits the corporations, and once again, the bankers who bankroll them.

Debt always requires that at some level, the world's natural resources be harvested and consumed, and this happens on such a vast scale that those irreplaceable resources are being constantly depleted.

In the process, we as consumers live within a system that is controlled at every level by central banks.

Regardless of what so-called economists might say, changing interest rates, as the Federal Reserve does from time to time, is in real terms nothing but a cover for keeping the world - and its people - in a state of mere survival.

True, a few become millionaires. Some become billionaires. But the vast majority spend their lives with their backs bent, their noses to the grindstone, making no financial progress whatever.

In reality, inflation does little or nothing to help anyone but the elite.

It keeps everyone else at a level of income that basically stays the same, because if you factor in a rise in personal income against the increase in inflation, which means rising prices, you are actually no better off at all.

Take a rise in gas prices as an example. Say you're earning $100 a week, and spending $10 on gas.

The price of gas goes up 10%, but your income, "adjusted for inflation" as they say (which is 2% on average for the country as a whole) only goes up to $102, out of which you must now find $11 for gas.

It doesn't seem like much, because you have that extra dollar in your pocket; but what you probably don't realize is that inflation (that $1 a week extra for gas) has literally stolen 50% of that 2% increase in your income. Further, a rise in gas prices leads to a rise in other prices, which means the more you earn, the more you spend; you never really get ahead.

Bottom line - inflation makes millions of people poorer, and a few thousand, just a few thousand, rich people get richer.

Whatever the rate of inflation, it is literally decreasing your purchasing power by that amount - which means your salary is worth less and less in real buying terms. That's why once upon a time a single person could earn enough to support a full family, but then both parties had to go to work in order to make ends meet, and now two full-timers can hardly make enough to cover the bills.

Vampires In Action

I won't name the banking insider, because he's a renegade from the system, and as I've said, they are ruthless. However, he does say there are only about 8000, maybe 8500 people at the top of the pyramid. And not one of them has a conscience.

He likens those at the top to "a bunch of vampires," and says as long as people do not realize what is going on, nothing will change, their business model that encompasses everything will continue, and all misery on Earth will remain unresolved.

That business model, as he calls it, encompasses the opium trade out of Afghanistan - now controlled by their surrogates since the US invasion of that country after 9/11. The invasion of Iraq was also a cover for gaining control of resources such as oil. The coup that was orchestrated in Ukraine in 2014 was intended to give companies such as Monsanto access to vast amounts of agricultural territory while at the same time setting up the ongoing confrontation with Russia and the expansion of NATO - which in turn benefits the military/industrial complex through the need for more weapons.

Oxfam International

Should there be any doubts about what Ramtha has had to say about the Rothschilds and the world's controllers which he has referred to at times over the past 40- years, especially in *"Last Waltz Of The Tyrants,"* a very current report about the world's wealthiest people should put those doubts to rest.

Oxfam International, whose slogan is "The Power of People Against Poverty," says in a press release that just eight men own the same amount of wealth as half the world.

They do not name the men, but the press release, headlined "An Economy for the 99 percent," says "big business and the super-rich are fueling the inequality crisis by dodging taxes, driving down wages and using their power to influence politics. It calls for a fundamental change in the way we manage our economies so that they work for all people, and not just a fortunate few."

Meanwhile, one in 10 people are surviving on less than $2 a day - and this has been going on for generations.

"The richest are accumulating wealth at such an astonishing rate that the world could see its first trillionaire in just 25 years. To put this figure in perspective - you would need to spend $1 million every day for 2738 years to spend $1 trillion.

"Public anger with inequality is already creating political shock waves across the globe. Inequality has been cited as a significant factor in the election of Donald Trump in the US, the election of President Duterte in the Philippines, and Brexit in the UK."

[The Oxfam website says it was formed in 1995 and is now "an international confederation of 20 organizations working together with partners and local communities in more than 90 countries.]

Whether they are named by Oxfam or not, the Rothschilds are among them, and possibly even richer than the eight that Oxfam doesn't name.

But there are thousands of others in the control seat as well. It's a control seat that could also be described as the seat of power. Global power. Power over politicians. Governments. Corporations. Nations. Institutions. And you and me.

All they have needed is money, and banks, and control of both, or, preferably, control of all banks everywhere, and through them, control of governments and the global financial system.

And so it goes on, and on, and on. Until it stops. But we'll get to that - after we hear some surprising truth from Ramtha once again.

Ramtha - They Have Souls

"There is not one grayman that is not endowed with God within them. They are not wicked in their souls. Their handmaidens are not wicked in their souls. They are by choice facilitating their image. The lust for power, which is the apex of the altered ego, is endless. It is not enough that they own the world's gold. It is not enough that they own all the fossil fuels under the earth. It is not enough that they destroy the rain forests for development. It is not enough that they pit one brother against another brother for the purpose of greed. That is power. The ultimate ejaculation of ecstasy for the image is to own the world and be its sovereign.

"These people are driven through heritage, through what they are fulfilling, their aims, their goals. Their goals are no different than yours. Yours are for sovereignty; theirs are for absolute power. It is the same energy. They have to fulfill it. It is their destiny. The ultimate for the altered ego is power and greed. Greed is the way you get it. A poor man can buy his respect in a twinkling of an eye when he soon becomes an heir.

"These people are forced into this. They hate one another because all of them want to be number one. They want to be in charge, so they hate one another, have violent wars between one another, and often thousands of people die over a dispute. They do not care. These entities in manifested destiny are coming to their ultimate victory march, for they have succeeded in their long-range plan up unto this hour, and to anyone who stood in their way, they did away with them and got them out of the picture. They are aligned and they are obsessed with their goals. The only thing that will eradicate this manifested destiny is knowledge and waking up. - Ramtha, *"Last Waltz of the Tyrants."* pp 53/54.

The Beast And The Card

Solon's Republic

We need only take a look at history, in another part of the world, in another time and place, to see what knowledge and waking up could look like.

In the days when Solon was elected Archon (the highest government administrative position) of Greece, about 2500 years ago, corn was grown and traded locally and in neighboring countries by local farmers.

The money lenders saw an opportunity here, and offered to loan the farmers money so they could plant more corn, make a bigger return, pay back the loan (with interest of course) and everyone would be happy.

Under the rules of the time, collateral was naturally required, and believe it or not, as well as putting up their land as part of the mortgage (or death pledge), the farmers would add themselves into the pot. If they couldn't repay what they'd borrowed, they could be sold off as slaves, leaving their wives and children homeless, while the money lenders now had ownership of the land.

By the time Solon became Archon, most of the land was in the hands of a small "aristocracy," who were now making an income through share-farming.

People who didn't own land or property themselves could farm the land, under a tight legal agreement of course, and the elite would harvest one-sixth of the annual income.

For the sake of simplicity, let's say that if the share-farmer spent a year working to make $10, the aristocratic owner/s - money lenders - would harvest one-sixth, or $1.66666666666667% of that $10 - without lifting a finger to do any of the manual labor at all.

Given the inclusion of all those 6's - there are 13 of them, which some would say is also significant - it's an interesting number indeed. Six six six. Six six six. Six six six. Six six six. six six seven percent.

A Bible Revelation

Maybe you've heard about it being in the Bible, in the Book of Revelation, which is what Ramtha refers to when talking about credit and debit cards.

Ramtha:- *"In your Book of Books there is a prophecy in Revelations - appropriate term - that wasn't tampered with. If you were John of old, the entity who prophesied hideous things in the last days, and an angel manifested a vision of a very big computer blinking at you — humming, turning, churning, ominous — and you had never seen one of these before, wouldn't you refer to it as a beast? Yes, of course you would. This entity saw through a vision of actual manifested destiny the climax of the very times you are living in, and the beast fed on a number, and the number be 666. The mark of the beast is represented by the beast embossing the number 666 through a tally of gold. Those who take this debit card will be owned and fortified with the beast and will have given up their liberty and freedom to their controllers. You give up absolute choice and freedom through it. When the vacuum becomes so severe that the vacuum collapses, the law of that collapse is change and those who take the card will be changed.*

"This is rightfully a prophecy of truth and it is on its way, rolling out in destiny, coming to pass." - Ramtha, *"Last Waltz Of The Tyrants,"* pp 54/55.

Let's check out the original quote in the Book of Revelation, as noted in this footnote on page 54 of Last Waltz of the Tyrants.

[Footnote, p 54:- "Verse 16 - And he causes all, the small and the great, and the rich and the poor, and the free men and the slaves, to be given a mark on their right hand or on their forehead, 17 - and he provides that no one will be able to buy or to sell, except the one who has the mark, either the name of the beast or the number of his name. 18 - Here is wisdom. Let him who has understanding calculate the number of the beast, for the number is that of a man; and his number is six hundred and sixty-six." - Revelation 13:16-18. New American Standard Bible.]

Going back to Greece, the situation was obviously, at least to Solon, an iniquitous one.

His people were losing their land, and families were losing their husbands and fathers, while the aristocracy continued to grow fat and lazy and richer and richer because they kept coming up with new schemes to increase their fortunes - always at the expense of the lower classes of course.

The money lenders saw nothing iniquitous at all in what they were doing. To them it was just business - cutthroat business but business nevertheless.

Now it is quite possible for a person to be both rich and happy, with a sense of morality that prohibits them from taking advantage of other people. They enjoy what they have, but they could also lose or walk away from every material possession and still be happy, because they are not owned by what they own.

Those are not the people we are referring to.

The other kind of rich, is rich, greedy, and unhappy. Unhappy because with greed comes a feeling of never having enough. This means then that such people are forever finding ways to add to what they have, by any means, and that means exploiting other people.

Such was the attitude of the aristocrats - the moneylenders - of Solon's time.

As prosperous as they had become by lending to the farmers, having gained much land through the sale into slavery of those men who couldn't repay their loans and thus adding their land to their list of assets, and then taking 6 per cent of a share farmers income ... all of that wasn't enough.

Adding to their concern was the fact that the few independent farmers who remained were either astute enough to borrow only what they were certain they could repay - or they borrowed nothing at all and were never in danger of losing their land, regardless of how good or bad a season might be.

This did nothing to appease the limitless greed that the money lenders were motivated by.

So what they did was, they started what we might call corporations, which in turn began importing corn which drove down the price of the local product, to the point that the Greek corn farmers went broke and were willing to sell their land just to survive.

This was a win-win-win for the elite.

Then along came Solon, saw the terrible plight of the homeless women and children, their husbands and fathers gone to slavery, those who were left as share-farmers paying a crippling percentage on their annual earnings, and he signed what we would call an executive order.

He just canceled all debt, and he told the elite "we're going to take back all that land, and we're going to buy back those farmers you sold into slavery as well. But here's the good news. You're going to be just as rich tomorrow as you were when you woke up this morning."

And with that stroke of genius and stroke of a pen he created Solon's Republic - after which the United States would eventually be modeled.

Unfortunately, this would not prevent the graymen from devising schemes that would not only ensure their survival, but also put them in control of what would become the next great would-be empire.

It's Not About The Money

Various forms of government have been tried throughout history, and by the time the Bauer/Rothschild family came along, the world had seen a succession of monarchs and empires with constantly shifting borders and endless battles and bloodshed and strife.

Not least among these was the era of the Crusades which were started and continued under the auspices of the Roman Catholic Church and its popes. It seems there has seldom if ever been a time when the various religions were not at odds with each other - as can be clearly seen in today's madness involving the three religions that all claim Abraham as their forefather.

However, religion was of no concern to the Rothschilds. Wars and crusades all cost money, and the Rothschilds quickly learned that they could profit most handsomely if they financed all sides of any dispute, with no allegiance to any state, monarch, religion, party or cause, except their own lust for power.

Ramtha - The Door To Power

As Ramtha put it when speaking of the first Rothschild:-

"To the image of this beginning grayman, the acquiring of wealth was the key that unlocked the door to power. It wasn't money that fulfilled this need, this image; it was power. This wonderful grayman soon realized on a return of his investment that he could work both sides against the middle, and he did." - Ramtha, *"Last Waltz of the Tyrants,"* p 25.

Brexit Bombshell

It was the ongoing imposition of austerity measures on the middle and working classes, the handouts to Big Business and Big Banks, the loss of jobs, and a continuing influx of migrants among other things that fueled the discontent, anger, and indeed hatred that saw 52 per cent in favor of leaving the European Union. That trumped the 48 per cent who wished to remain.

Subsequent to those events, we have seen the turmoil of the US presidential election, and eventually the election of Donald Trump as president. But the turmoil hasn't stopped. If anything, it has escalated - and behind it all there are indications that the unseen hand of the Rothschilds and other New World Order advocates is at work.

What we have to realize is that turmoil and chaos are harbingers of change - and unless the world changes for the better, those secretive controllers will indeed have their way.

Yet it seems they sense they are now on the back foot. Before we hit the 21st Century it was thought by some writers and bloggers that the Illuminati wanted to achieve their goal by the year 2000.

That didn't happen, and despite the tragic false flag of 9/11/2001- the controlled demolition of the Twin Towers in New York that was passed off as an attack by devout Muslims using box-cutter knives to hijack four plans - as well as the endless "war on terror" since then, instead of a unified world under one global government of the elite, we have a world divided against itself, but with no sign to date that the New World Order will indeed come about.

However, they do not give up, even though their dream is becoming more of a nightmare because they are losing control. On the surface this may not be obvious, especially since there is widespread ignorance about who has been pulling the strings from behind the scenes, so we see people venting their misplaced anger in serious and violent protests.

Meanwhile, most of the true villains remain hidden - except for those who live a double life, a life of lies and deception.

Those are the people in high places who have infiltrated politics, risen to the top in business and even established bogus charitable foundations, all intended to keep the wool pulled over the public's eyes.

Despite their best efforts, what a few years ago was just murmurings of discontent has blossomed into a growing rejection of the status quo, as seen in the Brexit vote in the UK, and the election of Donald Trump in the United States.

Hillary Clinton, who was the graymen's choice, did not make the cut. And that has put an end to the status quo whereby the Globalists were incrementally working toward their final goal, which is why the Cabal, the Illuminati, whatever they are called, are fighting back, and fighting dirty.

They want their version of the status quo to stay intact, because that means they can continue to protect each other and keep their corruption and dirty secrets covered up behind the facade of doing good, keeping people protected, keeping us all safe, and healthy, while their true intent is so very much the opposite.

How better to reveal just one aspect of that than in what Ramtha had to say about the Clinton Foundation and how the Clintons ripped off literally billions of dollars that had been donated to help those left alive after the devastating Haiti earthquake.

The winds of change are blowing - and as Trump's presidency evolves, those winds will no doubt reach hurricane strength.

Change Is Needed

Ramtha says:- *"If nothing else changes and everything continues status quo, there is no need to evolve. If there is no reason to change how everything is at the present time, nothing will change, and yet as hard as it has been to hear this, it needs change. The more you are aware of it, the more this consciousness exists. Ever hear of the old term supply and demand? A lot of demanding is going to go on very shortly. It creates the vacuum for the creators. That is purposeful, not direful."* - Ramtha, *"Last Waltz of the Tyrants,"* p 145.

Middle Class Misery

Sandwiched between the elite and the poor, we have a very much larger group within society. The Middle Class.

They are the workers, the taxpayers, the fountain of plenty which, whether they know it or not, is responsible through a plethora of taxes for helping the rich get richer while their money is also used to pay for government welfare programs that benefit those on the low end of the scale.

Governments love to take credit for their welfare programs and most recipients are grateful for what they receive, which may be seen in the way they vote for whoever has promised them the best deal.

But for the Middle Class it is a completely different story, since their money - if they have had any left after paying a zillion taxes on everything from their income to the hidden taxes associated with phone use, gas tax and so forth - has mostly been tied up in pension funds, retirement accounts, and mortgages or other debt.

For them, plunging stock markets and what looks like an inevitable Depression, because the graymen can instigate such things, means their upward mobility can suddenly see a rapid and in some cases instantaneous downward spiral.

"Ruining The World."

According to Ramtha, the graymen are ruining the world ...

He says:- *"It was easy to see how the banks, the carpetbaggers, the rascals, indeed the graymen could presume an initial goal of ruining the world through the monetary system and in the process break the back of the middle class, because as long as there is a middle class, democracy and the republic still stand. Elitism is threatened by your very existence and in your power and ability to be enlightened, and I am speaking of enlightenment not necessarily in regard to what is taught in the school system but an historical enlightenment whose works are available in most places to understand what really happened, not what you were told happened."* - Ramtha, *"Last Waltz of the Tyrants,"* p 112.

"By 1920 the graymen had grown to twelve families. They were the individuals who owned the international banks and literally Switzerland itself. They were the ones who incorporated that gold no longer be convenient to carry around. They were the ones who created paper money. They created the bank of London. They owned the bank of London. They created a major Federal Reserve in every major country where they printed money according to their desire and their plans for power." - Ramtha, *"Last Waltz of the Tyrants,"* p 31.

i

Look Back - Look Ahead

Now let's imagine it is the Christmas/New Year holiday season, making the break from 2016 to 2017.

The North Star Newsletter article of that date was headlined "Look Back, Then Look Forward," and the question was, "So What's Up For 2017?"

Since 1913, the graymen have used the power of money to effectively but surreptitiously control the US economy and many of its politicians. At will, they can make the stock market sink or swim, regardless of how many ordinary folk might drown in the process - or find themselves swimming in debt.

Past presidents, and Prime Ministers elsewhere, who have tried to free their people from debt have either been ridiculed out of office, or assassinated.

Presidents John Kennedy and Abraham Lincoln are two of the best-known examples of assassinations in America. But how many people know the reasons why Ronald Reagan was also the victim of an assassination attempt - which he fortunately survived?

According to Ramtha in Last Waltz of the Tyrants Reagan also wanted to create America's own independent bank and to print its own money.

Says Ramtha:- *"The entity struggled to bring to the surface through the media the creation of the American central bank, which would be the bank of the American people, endeavoring in his own way to create its own money. This was never fully investigated as his affairs were, and the entity that was to help him in this little matter was removed from his post. The name of that entity was Paul Volcker.*

"This president was one of three that in the final analysis will bring about Solon's republic — superconsciousness." - Ramtha, *"Last Waltz Of The Tyrants,"* p 41.

Ramtha did not name the other presidents he said would bring about the age of superconsciousness.

The graymen however have had a global reach for hundreds of years, and among their victims was a past Prime Minister of New Zealand, Richard Seddon - known back then as King Dick because of his autocratic attitude.

The official version is that "in June 1906, while returning from a trip to Australia on the ship Oswestry Grange, Seddon had a massive heart attack and died suddenly, 12 days before his 61st birthday."

Another version, (and here I deliberately use the term "from personally trusted sources" since there are two of them) is that King Dick was returning by ship from Australia to New Zealand after attending a conference where he revealed his plan to introduce a new monetary system for his country.

It would be independent of the Bank of England, which of course was the stronghold of the Rothschilds and their monetary stranglehold on the British Empire, of which New Zealand was a part.

These sources say that King Dick was murdered on his way home, most likely by poisoning.

Some quick research into how the Globalists might create heart attacks back then reveals that this could possibly have been an assassination using a salt substitute administered either in or on his meals. We won't reveal the ingredients here, but the combination causes heart attacks while leaving no clearly identifiable evidence of the cause.

There would definitely have been no forensic scientist in those days with access to blood samples, an analysis of which might have proved that this was murder. The finding that this was nothing other than a massive heart attack has therefore stood to this day.

Coming back to the present - 2017 - Donald Trump showed how feisty he can be during his election campaign, and since he's a life-long businessman who has survived and learned from hundreds of deals and several company bankruptcies, it'll be interesting to see how President Trump handles whatever pressures the graymen attempt to exert on him.

Donald Trump - Wild Card

Now we come to December 23, 2016, the date on which President Obama signed into law the updated National Defense Authorization Act.

Aside from funding the military and extending the provision that allows for arrest and incarceration without trial of anyone "suspected" of being associated with terrorism, something else was added but buried deep inside the legislation - the "Countering Disinformation and Propaganda Act."

The irony of this is that the US has for many decades engaged in its own form of disinformation and propaganda, both domestically and internationally, through outlets such as Voice of America, National Public Radio, the New York Times, the Washington Post and most if not all of the mainstream (fakestream) media.

It is another sign that the "graymen" are doing everything they possibly can to hold on to the reins of power - even though those reins are slipping through their fingers at an accelerating pace.

There is a policy in the establishment media of not reporting the many assassination threats that are made against the president, although they do mention the occasional event when it suits their agenda - their agenda being, in the case of Donald Trump, character assassination.

Independent assessments have shown that since Donald Trump's election, the mainstream media coverage has been up to 97 per cent negative.

That's why the mainstream media front has been filled with a constant barrage of fake news about Russia having hacked into the Democratic National Committee files and released emails to Wikileaks, which in turn supposedly released them on the Internet, which in turn (the mainstream media would have us believe) influenced the election campaign in favor of Donald Trump.

There's another way to look at this though, and that is, instead of seeing a conspiracy involving Russia and the Trump campaign, how about a conspiracy involving puppets of the graymen within both parties, in all of the US intelligence agencies, and the mainstream media - a conspiracy to discredit or obstruct the new president in every possible way.

You may recall the media reports that Trump was briefed by intelligence agencies which expressed what they called "a high degree of confidence" that Russia did what they say Russia did. And yet, they have also admitted that there is no way to say exactly how Russia's "interference" actually affected the election results.

Nor did they offer any specific proof at all that Russia was responsible for any hacking. They just claimed to have "a high degree of confidence," which really means nothing at all without facts and real evidence to back it up.

It was all a deliberate ploy.

With the puppet media and puppet journalists staying focused on the "Russia did it" meme, along with their "everyone else is fake news" claims - while they themselves propagate all the fake news they can make up about Russia - anything to do with the revelations in those emails about the Clinton Foundation or Clinton Charities or about an active pedophile and child-trafficking ring and other horrendous activities is effectively off the radar.

Such is the art of perception management by politicians, bureaucrats and the media.

They want us all to hate the president, and they're doing it using one of their assassination techniques. It's called character assassination.

Instead of getting sucked into their agenda, shouldn't we be thinking for ourselves, and asking ourselves, just who is this new president?

Before we get to a prophecy Ramtha made about President Donald Trump meeting UFOs, it would be prudent to look at the background of this man who is now the 45th president of the United States.

Now that he has shocked the graymen to the core by winning the election despite all the negative publicity, the manipulation of voting in the primaries, and the regular character assassination "leaks" that occurred, the new president is in the White House, and it looks like he's determined to stay.

As for his background, here's a shorthand version gleaned from the public record.

Donald Trump was born June 14, 1946, raised in Queens, New York City, enrolled in the New York Military Academy, in Cornwall, New York, at the age of 13, where he finished eighth grade and high school.

During his senior year he attained the rank of captain, then moved on to Fordham University in the Bronx for two years, then to the Wharton School of the University of Pennsylvania in Philadelphia, where he gained an economics degree at the age of 22 in 1968.

He took charge of his family's real estate and construction firm in 1975, and later renamed it The Trump Organization, which has built, renovated, and managed numerous office towers, hotels, casinos, and golf courses.

Starting at the age of 50, Trump owned the Miss USA and Miss Universe pageants, from 1996 to 2015.

From 2004 to 2015 he hosted The Apprentice, a reality television series on NBC where he became famous for his one-liner, "You're fired."

Court Cases and Bankruptcies

Looking at his legal affairs during the presidential campaign, the publication "USA Today" reported that over the previous three decades, Trump and his businesses had been involved in 3,500 legal cases in U.S. federal and state courts. Trump or one of his companies was the plaintiff in 1,900 and the defendant in 1,450.

About 500 cases against Trump were dismissed. He won 451 times, lost 38 - and the results of the rest are unclear as far as the public record goes.

In a BBC documentary made some years ago Trump admitted that at one point he was $900 million in debt and certainly on the verge of bankruptcy.

While his opponents have deliberately implied that Trump has been a bankrupt, he has never personally filed for bankruptcy.

Rather, his hotel and casino businesses have been declared bankrupt six times, perhaps done deliberately in order to re-negotiate debt with banks and owners of stocks and bonds.

Run For The White House

Over the years, Trump considered running for various political offices, but it wasn't until June 16, 2015, two days after his 69th birthday, by which time he was worth over $4 billion, that he announced his candidacy for the 2016 presidential election.

Trump paid much of the expenses of his campaign from his own fortune, and he now donates his presidential salary to various causes. He works as president for $1 a year.

At age 70, he is the oldest and wealthiest person to assume the presidency, and also the first without previous military or political experience. What he does have is a lifetime of experience as a businessman - a background that no previous president could match.

Hard Times And Dirty Tricks

The New York Times, which throughout the campaign was clearly biased against Trump, at one point wrote a story claiming that "some accountants considered Trump's tax deduction methods in the early 1990s 'legally dubious,' and 'sleight of hand.' "

Dirty tricks from a biased media have always been part of the election process, but the same goes for politicians themselves - they resort to every underhanded trick they can think of in their efforts to win votes.

Project Veritas, which produced a series of short election-related YouTube videos using under-cover methods, revealed that Clinton campaign insiders were deliberately setting up confrontational protests, including the use of clowns, and planning to bus Democrat voters interstate to boost her vote and poll numbers.

Although they would deny that they had any intention of influencing voters, publications like Politico, The Washington

Post, The New York Times, and the Los Angeles Times all took pleasure in running anti-Trump articles. All of them would claim they were simply pointing out what they termed as lies or falsehoods in Trump's campaign statements.

If that was true of Trump, it was equally true of the Clintons.

A record 84 million people watched the first debate between Donald Trump and Hillary Clinton, after which Trump's opponents went into overdrive, leaking a tape of Trump making lewd comments about women - for which he later apologized.

Trump responded in one of the next debates by telling an inconvenient truth - that Bill Clinton had not just made lewd comments about women. Trump said Bill Clinton had actually 'abused women' and that Hillary had "bullied her husband's victims."

Bill Clinton, he said, "was impeached and lost his license to practice law and paid an $850,000 fine to one of the women, Paula Jones."

Those who wish to split hairs, as attorneys and some journalists tend to do, point out that the $850,000 was not a fine, as Trump claimed, but a settlement, without Bill Clinton admitting liability as to the charge - which was one of harassment in that he (Clinton) had exposed himself to Jones in a hotel room in 1991.

The way the US electoral system is set up, the final decision on who gets to be president is made by what's known as the Electoral College. While Hillary Clinton won the popular vote (and there are questions about whether that was achieved by devious means), Trump won the decisive Electoral College vote.

That was an absolute shock to the Globalists who had done everything they could to ensure Hillary Clinton would be elected.

Nevertheless, she and her political machine were not about to go quietly. Instead, they were planning every conceivable way to discredit and destroy the man who had thrown a monkey wrench into their Globalist plans.

That was when the Democrats and their allies in high places came up with the "Russia Interfered" and "Russia and Trump" smear campaign.

Smear By Smut

Something very strange happened just prior to the inauguration, and here again we may sense the presence of the graymen and their puppets. In early January, Trump was briefed by top intelligence agency officials, including the then head of the CIA, on allegations that Russia had "potentially compromising personal and financial information" about him.

A private intelligence dossier was later leaked to the media and to the public containing the claims. Some of the material alleged dubious sexual and financial conduct by Trump, and reporter Bob Woodward called the unsubstantiated dossier a "garbage document" meriting an apology from whoever wrote and leaked it.

Keep in mind that character assassination is one of the tools of politicians everywhere, but it has proven particularly useful in the past for the Globalist/New World Order people who have been very careful about putting their own followers into positions of power, and not just as politicians, prime ministers or presidents. Many of them are the people who make up The Deep State, being in positions of power within various government departments where they usually have long-term tenure.

Many of them can be found within the media and government agencies, especially the intelligence community.

Leaking that totally unsubstantiated document with all its salacious lies and the ensuing media frenzy no doubt harmed Trump's image in the eyes and minds of many, which it was intended to do.

And then came the inauguration.

But first, let's look at two incidents involving President Trump and UFOs.

The Ramtha Trump Prophecy
UFOs And The President-elect

The day before his inauguration, president-elect Donald Trump was flown in a military aircraft from New York to Washington DC.

Naturally, the event was covered by the mainstream media, including Fox News.

They had a film crew up in another plane, filming the aircraft leaving New York and heading for Washington DC.

Where it got really interesting was that after the footage was aired, one of those "alternative media" people analyzed the footage and discovered one or more UFOs were also in the vicinity of that big military aircraft.

The YouTube introduction said "Another UFO was seen near Trump, but this time it was seen nearly colliding with the jet itself. As you can see the UFO shot past at such a speed even the camera had difficulty focusing on it. Fox News was lucky enough to catch it and show it on national TV today. It looks like Fox News has found proof that aliens have a deep interest in Americas new president and what he has destined for the world."

This is where we jump backwards to December 8, 2016 - about six weeks before this happened. On that date, that evening, Ramtha was being channeled by JZ Knight at Ramtha's School of Enlightenment (RSE) in Yelm, Washington. He was talking about what is to come in 2017 and the years ahead.

After the UFO incident involving President Trump, RSE posted a transcript on its newsletter website - a part of what Ramtha had to say that night - and it was all about Donald Trump and UFOs.

The RSE article introduction reads:- *"December 8, 2016, Ramtha Predicted that UFOs Would Trail President Trump's Plane and Described the Significance of these Coming Events for Disclosure ..."*

The following words are what Ramtha said ...

"The first time he looks out the window of his mighty-fine, used-but-nice jet and sees two silver discs waving beside him as an escort, he is going to know it all. This is a man who is not afraid. He is going to know it all. Not only will he learn about the energy systems that have been kept from the American people and the world, used exclusively for the military and the privileged, he is going to expose it all. He had no problem doing what he has just done. He is fearless. He is fearless, because he is an optimist. He knows there is more that can be made. Do you understand?"

"You will learn that there are other alien civilizations. The whole world will learn it." - Ramtha, December 8, 2016, Yelm, WA.

Next, we need to get the man - Donald Trump - the rogue elephant - inaugurated.

The Inauguration Speech

Because it is better to allow people to do their own analyzing and form their own conclusions, after the inauguration the North Star Newsletter simply offered subscribers the full text of Donald Trump's speech, and also invited written reactions.

We'll get to some of those, but first, some of the more significant statements from that speech:-

"Today's ceremony," said the incoming president, "has very special meaning because today we are not merely transferring power from one administration to another or from one party to another, but we are transferring power from Washington, D.C. and giving it back to you, the people.

"For too long, a small group in our nation's capital has reaped the rewards of government while the people have borne the cost. Washington flourished, but the people did not share in its wealth.

"Politicians prospered, but the jobs left and the factories closed. The establishment protected itself but not the citizens of our country."

"That all changes starting right here and right now, because this moment is your moment. It belongs to you. It belongs to everyone gathered here today and everyone watching all across America."

"This is your day, this is your celebration, and this, the United States of America, is your country."

We will no longer accept politicians who are all talk and no action constantly complaining but never doing anything about it.

"The time for empty talk is over. Now arrives the hour of action.

"We stand at the birth of a new millennium ready to unlock the histories (mysteries) of space, to free the earth from the miseries of disease and to harness the energies, industries and technologies of tomorrow.

"Together we will make America strong again. We will make America wealthy again. We will make America proud again. We will make America safe again.

"And, yes, together, we will make America great again."

Reader comments

Everyone is entitled to their own interpretation - and the following comments from subscribers to the North Star Newsletter appear to cover the gamut.

First:- "How you (and Ramtha) can support this man, makes me think I'm living in the twilight zone or on another planet. He may be a shrewd businessman (which is open to question) and not a "politician" but where is his heart?

"He is thin skinned, arrogant, combative, bombastic and uses adjectives that have no meaning. He has deliberately divided this country and is the only President who has never revealed his tax returns.

"He will give new meaning to the word "nepotism" and doesn't expect it to apply to him and having his family in his inner circle to give him advice and support. After all, they have proven their undying loyalty to him so he doesn't have to tweet about them.

"How can you ignore what you see in this man's face and countenance? He has now become King Trump and expects everyone in Washington (and the world) to bow down to him. He has handed out cabinet posts to those who have supported him and who, in most cases, are poorly, if at all, qualified for their positions.

"He boasts that he has no interest in understanding history nor has he read any biographies of past presidents since he wants to do the most powerful job in the world "his way".

"He plans to dismantle the Environmental Protection Agency at a time when our planet is fighting back against the one species set on destroying its habitat. He is repealing the Affordable Care Act and potentially leaving 20 million + Americans without health care...the only civilized western country leaving its citizens so vulnerable.

"Here are my final thoughts. Like everyone else in this country, I'm waiting to see if this man can deliver on his promises without destroying Medicare and Medicaid, without alienating our allies in the rest of the world and without starting WWIII.

"Maybe he can bring jobs back to America. Maybe he can do something about the Student Loan crisis. And maybe, just maybe, I can be proven wrong about him. I welcome that day indeed." - J.

Next:- "I thought this a great speech, but I took it for what he said, not [what he did not] say. I did not vote for Trump but he is our President and we have to support him and, with luck and the support of the great Brotherhood, he will make it. I just wish he would put Twitter away, act like an adult and not a spoiled child on occasions.

"The reality in this country is hate and division, and it is only time, and his leadership of openness, not pettiness, that will prevail. He certainly has upset the voters with his rhetoric and behavior, but he is our leader and we have to help him. "Good luck Mr. Trump.

"One thought though, I wish the Party would stop being so hypocritical and maybe he would make Mitch an ambassador in Kenya. Politics as usual?" (Name withheld by request.)

This is from Liz:- "Whatever made you think I would want to waste time reading that. Just a few of the excerpts on TV were more than enough. It sends cold (very cold) shivers up my spine, and all through me for that matter."

Next:- "Trump reminds me of Ram in that both are wonderfully honest, and neither is afraid to speak the name of God." E.

And this one:- "These words from Trump are so beautiful, and contain within an evocative indication of what our teacher predicted. I very much appreciate the chance you gave me to read every word of our new President's speech." - RT.

And this:- "Oh yay what a great speech. So much in there behind the words as well." - D.

Another:- "T'is a grand day in America! He nailed it." - S.

From N and H:- "Thank You for posting the acceptance speech Michael. We each and all are hopeful there is some cognizance happening."

Sandra had this to say:- "I saw it and I am glad he is not a politician. He is a rogue per our teacher, let's hear it for change. I like it that Robert Kennedy Jr. is part of his team."

And then there was this comment on the Internet:- "I must say, his speech was awesome !! He ripped DC a new one… Let's hope he is true to his word !!"

This one is from The Yelm Community Blog:- "Serving as Yelm's Democratic Area Caucus Coordinator (ACC) in March 2016 and a devotee Bernie Sanders liberal, I salute and congratulate the 45th President of the United States, Donald J. Trump!

"He IS this country's President and laid out a clear vision from where we have come, where we are, and his vision of the way forward - the time has arrived for America being used as a pawn by "The Establishment" for world domination to end today!

"America First" - A new day for our country begins now!

"Blessings to The President, his family, and team!

"And THANK YOU to President Obama and his family for their service to our country!" -*Steve Klein*

As for my personal take, having covered a national election in the past and therefore being quite familiar with the workings of politics ... a great speech, yes, however it is also said that actions speak louder than words, so I trust (and I do) that we will see actions that back up those words."

Press Responses

While millions of supporters either attended or were watching the inauguration of President Donald Trump, there was the usual instant plethora of mainstream talking heads and media commentators ready and willing to dissect what he had to say.

Perhaps I have my own bias, or at least am somewhat jaundiced when it comes to today's press coverage, especially on this occasion, which is such an important event in world terms.

A man has just been sworn in as the leader of what is seen to be the most powerful nation in the world, and his opponents, especially those in the mainstream press, immediately begin to tear him apart.

It's easy to spot the bias of the media when you see such headlines as *"Analysis - Raw, angry and aggrieved, President Trump's inaugural speech does little to heal political wounds."*

That was in the LA Times and it is just one example of many of today's so-called mainstream writers.

They have long ago given up being journalists guided by impartiality. Rather, they themselves engage in writing opinionated pieces, as if their opinions are a genuine reflection of public opinion in general, when in reality they are serving that "deep state" agenda of perception management.

What we don't need to be reminded of is that today's western media, not only in America, but throughout Europe and Britain and much of the rest of the world, is owned and controlled by the Cabal - by corporations that have their footing in that New World Order pipe dream.

Rot In The System

Watergate To Pizzagate

Forty three years ago - in 1974 - President Nixon was forced to resign in what has become known as the Watergate scandal - a break-in to the Democratic Party's offices at the Watergate complex two years earlier in Washington DC, 1972.

It transpired that Nixon and his associates were using the FBI, the CIA and the IRS to target political opponents as well as bugging their offices.

If that scenario sounds familiar, it's because it is. President Obama was accused of using the IRS to target individuals and groups as well, and President Trump has also charged the Democrats with having wiretapped his conversations during the election campaign last year.

Politics obviously hasn't changed much in the past 40 years or so - in fact, if anything, things are worse these days than they ever were.

Nixon resigned in August 1974, to be replaced by Gerald Ford, who pardoned Nixon just four weeks later.

Washington Post reporters Bob Woodward and Carl Bernstein are credited with uncovering much of the cover-up, referring to one of their sources as "Deep Throat."

Since then it has been suggested that Woodward and Bernstein might have been used by "Deep Throat" who years later was revealed to be the then deputy director of the FBI - William Mark Felt Sr.

The suggestion is that Felt, aka Deep Throat, was an operative for the Cabal - the New World Order - which wanted Nixon out of office because he had in a sense gone off the reservation. He was angling toward becoming president of the One World Government, once it was established, but on his own terms rather than following the Cabal's agenda.

Whether that's true or not, Nixon was ousted, and variations on the term Watergate have been used ever since in regard to various scandals, one of the latest being referred to as Pizzagate.

The term was coined because of hints in Hillary Clinton's election campaign emails that many in "the Establishment" are involved in child abuse and sex trafficking.

That story has been buried by the mainstream media as "fake news" while they themselves, aided and abetted by the FBI and CIA and other intelligence agencies have focused on denigrating the new president with fake claims that Russia somehow influenced the election, and that Trump and his associates are pawns of Russia's President Putin.

If you've been involved in the media for over 50 years, and personally witnessed the way politicians deceive each other and the people they are supposed to represent, you find yourself wondering - suspecting - that these Pizzagate allegations are actually well founded, and that people in high places - and we're talking both parties as well as those in the "deep state" - actually fear being exposed as criminals now that an outsider, Donald Trump, holds the reins of power.

Pedophilia, child abuse, mind control and sex trafficking are nothing new in this world, and such activity is not confined to the halls of power.

Unfortunately, it is those in power who are best able to get away with it, since they make the laws while for the most part being above the law.

They are able to placate the public by calling for investigations into serious issues, while controlling the outcome of such investigations, as they have done on multiple occasions.

We don't have to go back too far to find examples either.

VERY False Flag - 9/11

The most egregious would be the inquiry into the events of 9/11/2001 when the world was stunned by the demolition (should I have said "collapse"?) of the Twin Towers in New York City.

The official line still insists that a group of Muslims, some of them trained on small planes in Florida, managed to use tiny box cutter knives to overcome the passengers and crew of four huge jetliners and successfully fly two of them into the towers, one into the Pentagon, and the fourth into a field in Pennsylvania.

Thousands of professional engineers, physicists and pilots and demolition experts have since shown that those towers could not possibly have come down unless it was a controlled demolition, planned well in advance. Nor did the official inquiry ever explain how Building Seven also collapsed in its own footprint in a matter of seconds - despite never having been hit by a plane at all.

On the day, a BBC reporter did a piece to camera saying WTC7 had also collapsed - while the building could be seen behind her, still standing. [More detail at Architects and Engineers for 9/11 Truth.] Yet that tragic day was the springboard for the ensuing wars in Afghanistan and Iraq, which in turn has seen Libya and now Syria being destroyed by America and its allies...all based on lies.

Another example - the Warren Commission inquiry into the assassination of President Kennedy in 1963. A lone gunman, Lee Harvey Oswald, is said to have taken three shots from a distance at the head of a man in a moving car. Oswald himself was subsequently assassinated by Jack Ruby before he could stand trial.

In 1979 a US House Select Committee on Assassinations actually disagreed with the Warren Commission report, concluding on the basis of multiple gunshots to be heard in a recording made on the day of the assassination that more than one gunman was involved, and that Kennedy was "probably assassinated as a result of a conspiracy." But that finding too was buried by the Justice Department when it insisted there was "no persuasive evidence to support the theory of a conspiracy."

There are many other examples of false flag events and government lies that have taken America to war or have been used by the power elite to impose ever-increasing restrictions on privacy, security and free speech in America.

Like it or not, the fact remains that the mainstream media plays a huge part in helping the government (or should we say "shadow government") achieve its goals, whether it's a matter of persuading the populace that war is vital, or in diverting public attention from scandals like Pizzagate by focusing on fake issues such as the claim that Russia influenced the presidential election of 2016.

This is why the mainstream media is no longer trusted by people who think for themselves - and why CNN should be seen as the Cabal News Network.

Rampant Decadence

Meanwhile, decadence runs rampant through the halls of power - but not only there. Decadence has become a world-wide phenomenon, and that is a sign that a so-called civilization has ceased to make any progress at all in terms of evolution.

For reasons explained in the various books that record Ramtha's teachings verbatim, numerous past civilizations have reached a pinnacle of evolution, only to become riddled with violence and decadence to the point that no further evolution was possible.

Unfortunately, given the state of this world at present, with its constant wars, and the many cover-ups surrounding such things as widespread pedophilia, not only in the Catholic church world-wide but also within the ranks of the elite, as well as the widespread eugenics (depopulation) efforts of the New World Order cartel, it is reasonable to wonder how close this civilization is to its own demise.

Ramtha - Sodom and Gomorrah

Ramtha:- "*When the mind stops learning and the Spirit no longer is engaged, the physical being is run by its hormones. It becomes decadent. That becomes its reality. Sodom and Gomorrah were also destroyed by an atomic blast from such a great ship. That happened in a twinkling of an eye. Why? How low does the human Spirit have to come that they engage sexual intercourse with the cattle of the field as a religious rite? You don't learn anymore. That has to be separated out and that seed removed so that the continuation of evolution can continue.* - Ramtha, "*UFOs and the Nature of Reality: Preparing for Contact,*" p 55.

It's a bit sick, but in 2012 the Huffington Post was running a story about a loophole in Florida law "that allows for certain forms of oral sex between humans and animals." Oddly enough, it was just a year prior to that, in 2011, that Florida actually outlawed bestiality.

Add to that the many reports of pedophile and sex trafficking operations around the world, including the involvement of men from various Christian denominations, and we have a current scenario that in many ways mirrors what was happening in the times of Sodom and Gomorrah.

Quoting Ramtha again:- *"If it is hard for you to hear about the destruction of Sodom and Gomorrah or Antusian and Elamon, then you are not ready to hear everything there is to know, which means that you do not have the mind capacity to go further than that because you are emotionally blocked. That is all right. You will learn what you are capable of learning and you will see only what you are capable of seeing."* - Ramtha, *"UFOs and the Nature of Reality: Preparing for Contact,"* p 72.

Anything BUT The Truth

President Trump wants to put a stop to illegal immigration, pull the United States back from being the world's policeman, if not close then at least put strict controls on the borders, do what he can to improve relationships with other countries, scrap various trade treaties that have cost Americans their jobs, and above all put America First.

As this is written, six months into his presidency, there is good reason to question whether he has really done much along those lines.

He has visited Saudi Arabia and closed some billion-dollar arms deals, gone to Poland and made a speech that made most NATO members reasonably happy, pulled out of the Paris climate accord, and met Russia's President Putin at the G20 gathering. Plus he has budgeted something like $1.5 billion for a wall across the border with Mexico - as well as re-establishing the National Space Council.

Despite all that, it's early days yet, but it is his declared "America First" policy that the Globalists fear, because nationalism is what their agenda is determined to do away with.

However, it is beginning to look like that plan is in serious jeopardy because Donald Trump, the wild card they obviously didn't expect to win the game, came along, got elected, and in doing so threw a wrench in their bicycle wheel.

In addition, revelations by the likes of Edward Snowden about NSA spying, and now the release by Wikileaks of over 8000 CIA documents with details about their cyber-weapons that are deployed to spy on anyone, anywhere, all the time, are further signs that the carefully constructed NWO plot is coming to light.

Ramtha:- *"The graymen are struggling and endeavoring to keep the plan suppressed. Blessed be the person who has spoken the truth, and there are many of them speaking the truth that know not I."* - Ramtha, *"Last Waltz of the Tyrants,"* p 90.

What we should all be well aware of by now is that the Cabal, the Globalists, would rather have us believe anything *but* the truth.

We can prove that with a quick look at their track record.

During the Bush/Cheney administration, the case was being made, with the help of a compliant mainstream press, for war against Iraq.

To sell the idea to the American public, and the so-called "coalition of the willing" in other countries, the administration came up with a game plan that involved hammering on the theme that Iraqi president Saddam Hussein was a butcher, and he had "weapons of mass destruction," including bio-warfare weapons, and was planning to build or use nuclear weapons.

They publicly claimed that he had been seeking yellowcake uranium from Niger, and that he had aluminum tubes that could be used for uranium enrichment. This was false, and it was contradicted by Joseph Wilson, a diplomat and husband of a woman named Valerie Plame. Wilson wrote an op-ed saying there was no evidence that Hussein had been seeking uranium.

To discredit and stop Wilson and others from questioning their push for war, the administration let it be publicly known that Wilson's wife, Valerie Plame, was a covert CIA officer, thereby destroying her future career.

In other words, she was "outed."

As for "outing," this is what Wikileaks has now done to the CIA itself, with its revelations that "the CIA (has) lost control of the majority of its hacking arsenal including malware, viruses, trojans, weaponized 'zero day' exploits, remote control systems and associated documentation."

Wikileaks said "This extraordinary collection, which amounts to more than several hundred million lines of code, gives its possessor the entire hacking capacity of the CIA.

"The archive appears to have been circulated among former U.S. government hackers and contractors in an unauthorized manner, one of whom has provided WikiLeaks with portions of the archive."

What this means is that the CIA's hacking arsenal could now be in the hands of "rival states, cyber mafia and teenage hackers alike."

Imagine that. A teenager, or a foreign enemy power, having the entire hacking capacity of the CIA.

It's as if those movies and TV series in which you see hackers at work prying into phone calls, bank accounts, criminal backgrounds, military service, even health files, as well as tracking good guys and bad guys using GPS signals from their cell phones, are indeed reflecting the real world.

And they do.

But it gets worse. Wikileaks went on to say-

"By the end of 2016, the CIA's hacking division, which formally falls under the agency's Center for Cyber Intelligence (CCI), had over 5000 registered users and had produced more than a thousand hacking systems, trojans, viruses, and other weaponized malware."

This is some of what those CIA geeks, or anyone who now has those programs, can do.

Put your smart TV (Samsung is named) in "fake off" mode while it continues recording your conversations and sending info back to the CIA.

Hack and control smart phones (geolocation, texts, audio, camera, microphone).

Infest, control and exfiltrate (send to the spying center) data from iPhones and other Apple products running iOS, such as iPads.

A similar unit targets Google's Android which is used to run the majority of the world's smart phones (~85%) including Samsung, HTC and Sony.

Bypass the encryption of WhatsApp, Signal, Telegram, Wiebo, Confide and Cloackman.

The CIA has developed automated multi-platform malware attack and control systems covering Windows, Mac OS X, Solaris, Linux and more.

The report adds that "As of October 2014 the CIA was also looking at infecting the vehicle control systems used by modern cars and trucks. The purpose of such control is not specified, but it would permit the CIA to engage in nearly undetectable assassinations."

Death By Hacking

Liars need to cover their tracks, and any advocate of truth who gets in their way is going to become a target, sometimes for character assassination - sometimes for death by assassination.

In the more than 100 years since New Zealand's King Dick died of an induced heart attack, the graymen's arsenal has definitely kept up with the times.

From global surveillance of computer and phone traffic, to the ability to remotely take control of computers installed in the latest vehicles, they have a wealth of options available. And they use them when it suits their agenda.

Remote controlled drones are basically flying computers that have been operated from a distance to kill hundreds, perhaps thousands, of innocent people in recent years. The thing about computers however, whether flying or not, is that they can be hacked.

But you probably knew that from watching television or the movies, right? Truth is, in the real world, that capability has existed for years, and it is thought to have been used to kill at least one independent journalist.

"In 2013, investigative journalist Michael Hastings, who was probing abuses by the CIA and NSA and had recently informed others that he was being investigated by federal authorities, died in a highly suspicious car crash in Los Angeles, California.

"Authorities officially ruled the death an accident, but serious questions began surfacing right away - even in the establishment media and among prominent officials.

"His friends said he normally drove 'like a grandma.' And yet, officially, according to the investigation, Hastings ran through a red light while supposedly driving more than 100 miles per hour in a crowded residential neighborhood before plowing into a tree and blowing up his car. The engine of his new Mercedes was found more than 150 feet away from the wreck."

Hastings was incinerated.

A year later, former CIA and NSA boss Michael Hayden would say "We kill people based on metadata."

How is it that an organization such as the CIA can boast about killing people, and get away with it? Let's think about that, and again consider something Ramtha had to say in *"Last Waltz of the Tyrants."*

"In 1857, throughout Europe, other places around the world, and the beginning of this country, the Rothschild dynasty had placed those individuals in important decision-making positions who were beholden to or in allegiance with this family."- Ramtha, *"Last Waltz of the Tyrants,"* p 27.

From that statement, one might deduce that "important decision-making positions" would not only include politicians, but also members of various government departments and agencies, such as the intelligence services.

Being "beholden to or having allegiance" to the ongoing New World Order agenda, would put them in perfect positions to incrementally bring about that goal - regardless of how many wars might be needed to convince the ill-informed masses that they should welcome a One World Government, or how many of their opponents they might assassinate, either literally, or figuratively - as has been happening with the ongoing campaign against President Trump and his family.

Warrantless Surveillance

What Wikileaks has revealed about the CIA is that it has been engaged in surveillance in multiple ways, without ever seeking a warrant for what it does.

Whether it was the CIA or some other alphabet agency that tapped into the Trump Tower during the election campaign we can't be sure about, but President Trump is definitely sure that it happened.

We also know that it was the intelligence community that kept beating the drum about links between Trump and Putin, and they too leaked a document accusing Trump of despicable behavior on a visit to Moscow.

Here Comes The Judge

The outspoken Judge Napolitano appeared on the Fox News Lou Dobbs show to discuss President Trump's statement that the Trump tower was wiretapped during the election campaign.

Following is a transcript of what the judge had to say about the Deep State.

"It has been around for many many years. Since 1947. The 'Deep State;' the part of the government that never changes no matter which party controls Congress and which party is in the White House.

"There are many many aspects of the Deep State.

"We're talking about the intelligence community that have access to so much information about everyone they can manipulate the President of the United States.

"And if they don't like what he says, they can embarrass him. If they want to control his thought patterns and decision making they'll keep information away from him.

"Donald Trump has fallen victim to that, and he knows it, and he knows he has to stop it.

"His suggestion for a Congressional investigation of the intelligence community is the last thing his enemies in the intelligence community want, because if the American public learns that they have access to everything we type, and everything we say, they will be repulsed by the power that this Deep State group has... that Congress gave them!

"They didn't create this on their own.

"Congress enacted three pieces of legislation which with perverse interpretations of this legislation before a secret court lets them gather everything we say in real time."

Napolitano went on to say "One of the FISA court warrants that I saw was quote 'for every customer of Verizon in the United States.'

"That's 113 million people. Including most of the Federal government."

Says Judge Napolitano:- "It's the first time in the modern era that the man in the Oval office has been an adversary of the Deep State, rather than a tool of it."

Trump And The Swamp

Given the almost totally negative tone of the mainstream media coverage of President Trump's first 100 days in office, one could get the impression that he is really unfit to be president, and that he will be ousted very soon either by an internal coup, or through impeachment.

Because the media, many politicians, and numerous bureaucrats and pundits keep hammering on the theme that Russia interfered in the election, that Trump's campaign staff are under investigation, or that he fired FBI Director James Comey in order to influence that investigation, it's natural for some to question Ramtha's prophecy that says in essence that Trump is the right man in the right place at the right time.

It's worth reviewing that prophecy of December 8, 2016 in which Ramtha said UFOs would ride alongside Trump's plane, and he would "know it all."

Ramtha - Trump Prophecy

"The first time he looks out the window of his mighty-fine, used-but-nice jet and sees two silver discs waving beside him as an escort, he is going to know it all. This is a man who is not afraid. He is going to know it all. Not only will he learn about the energy systems that have been kept from the American people and the world, used exclusively for the military and the privileged, he is going to expose it all. He had no problem doing what he has just done. He is fearless. He is fearless, because he is an optimist. He knows there is more that can be made. Do you understand?"

"You will learn that there are other alien civilizations. The whole world will learn it."- Ramtha, December 8 2016, Yelm, WA.

Knee Deep In S..wamp

People who are on Trump's side use the phrase "draining the swamp," the swamp being a metaphor for Washington DC.

They may not be aware of the underlying New World Order agenda that is the tie that binds many of the swamp dwellers together in some sort of fraternity of the ungodly, but they are certainly aware that Trump is surrounded by enemies.

Every move he makes is subjected to the spin that the mainstream media, the Democrats and even some members of the Republican party, as well as trolls on the Internet, are adept at. Their belief is that if they work hard enough at influencing public opinion, at some point Trump will either cave and resign, or he will be ousted in some other way and the public won't give a damn.

Ramtha - Reagan One Of Three

Many years ago Ramtha said of President Ronald Reagan that he would be one of three who would lead America to the return of Solon's Republic.

In addition, Ramtha said:- *"He was a great man. There is also another reason why this entity was there. He was not completely the puppet of the anonymous graymen. You will never see the graymen getting their faces in papers. You won't hear anything about them. They remain anonymous. They choose that. It is the best for business. This president also had within him a great love for God and righteousness. "*- Ramtha, *"Last Waltz Of The Tyrants,"* p 40.

"This president was one of three that in the final analysis will bring about Solon's republic — superconsciousness. For those of you who do not know, I do not vote and I do not campaign. My daughtren quoted the great writer Cicero who spoke truth when he said, 'Politicians aren't born; they are excreted.' President Reagan

was endeavoring to hold together the last throes of trying to do the right thing, not knowing how to go about it, and this was bearing upon his consciousness." - Ramtha, *"Last Waltz Of The Tyrants,"* p 41.

Ramtha did not name the other two presidents that would bring about the Solon's Republic that he referred to. However his prophecy about Donald Trump does suggest that Trump is one of those three.

Whatever his faults might be, this wildcard president is certainly no-one's puppet either.

Remember, in his inauguration speech he said:- "Today's ceremony, however, has very special meaning. Because today we are not merely transferring power from one Administration to another, or from one party to another - but we are transferring power from Washington, D.C. and giving it back to you, the American People."

We add italics to the next quote from his address to give it a little emphasis:- *"For too long, a small group in our nation's Capital has reaped the rewards of government while the people have borne the cost. That all changes - starting right here, and right now, because this moment is your moment: it belongs to you."*

Taking into account a population of over 300 million in the United States, that "small group in the Nation's Capital," is minuscule. Yet it would be safe to say that their numbers are likely in the hundreds, and probably in the thousands if we think globally.

As well, they are assisted by media conglomerates, in particular the New York Times, which frequently quotes unnamed sources - sources which then say something derogatory about the president, or refer to the "Russian influence." All of which is a series of lies started and perpetuated by the Democrats who lost the election.

The Washington Post is equally guilty, if not more so, but few seem to recall that that "news" paper is owned by Jeff Bezos, founder of Amazon, who received a $600 million CIA contract just after he bought the Washington Post in 2013.

The New York Post is also in on the spin, with reprint articles (from the New York Times) which make claims such as "President Trump told Russian officials who visited the Oval Office that ousted FBI director James Comey "was crazy, a real nut job" and that canning him took "great pressure" off of him, a new report said Friday.

"I just fired the head of the FBI. He was crazy, a real nut job," Trump said, according to a document that summarized the sitdown, the New York Times reported."

Documents can be written by anyone, and especially by corrupt reporters, among whom there are numerous individuals with ties to the various intelligence agencies.

Not once have any of Trump's accusers, or any of the media with access to all their unnamed sources "speaking on condition of anonymity" come up with any real evidence of Russia influencing the election.

And yet the allegations and innuendo continue unabated.

Worse still, not once as far as we can find has any journalist asked the simple questions:- "Where and precisely what evidence is there?

"Where is your definitive proof that Russia hacked into the DNC systems as you have claimed? In what way, and precisely how, did you identify this 'influence' that you claim cost Hillary Clinton the election?"

What's Not In The News

Fixated as it is on the "Russia did it" meme, the western press gives only passing mention to subjects that in an honest media world be cause for major and ongoing investigation and exposure.

The murder of Seth Rich, the Democratic National Committee insider who purportedly leaked information to Wikileaks is one example.

He was shot twice in the back while out walking one dark night in Washington DC. The Democrats would express their sadness about his death, but continue to claim those leaks were the result of a Russian hack, and that's how the "Russia did it" cover story got started.

The "Pizzagate" story - the one that suggests there are pedophiles in high places within the DNC (and both parties, according to *"Trance:Formation of America,"*) has also been buried by the mainstream media, although they have had little option but to at least run one story that tells us just how vast this network is.

The headline was "Massive Pedophile Ring Busted; 230 Kids Saved." It was about an Internet pedophile ring with up to 70,000 members. It was one of those subjects the legacy media simply could not avoid, and yet there is no serious follow-through.

What they don't seem to know, or are not yet prepared to reveal, is that there are people in both parties, and entrenched within the military, intelligence agencies and law enforcement, who believe in the creation of a New World Order, with themselves being among the elite, and Donald Trump and the rest of us nowhere in sight.

Silent War Within America

It's June 2017 and recent Internet articles are pointing to a "summer of rage" in the United States.

How this will play out remains to be seen, but one could easily come to the conclusion - the shocking conclusion - that America itself is under siege.

It is under siege by what may be described as The UnAmerican Americans.

They have planned so well that all the signs are pointing toward a coup that will give its adherents total control of this country. Or so they hope.

Calls for the impeachment of President Trump are just one part of this coup strategy.

However, it is not only President Trump they are after. Yes, they certainly want to get him out of office, and they may even succeed in doing so, but their designs for the future go much further than that, as does their record of past and successful coup achievements.

To explain this, and what it could mean when it comes to this "summer of rage" we need to take at least a brief look at what we are told is Democracy in America, and coups that America has created around the world since at least 1953.

"The disquieting reality of the world we live in is that American efforts to destroy democracy, even as it pretends to champion it, have left the world less peaceful, less just and less hopeful."

That sentence is taken from a lengthy article titled "America's Coup Machine: Destroying Democracy Since 1953" at www.alternet.org.

Decrying The President

That website comes with a lot of articles decrying President Trump, saying he "might just have doomed human civilization once and for all," to "we have a deviant in the White House," to "does Vladimir Putin own Donald Trump? It's more likely than you think."

Obviously, those headlines are just part of the 97% of current Trump coverage that is as anti-Trump as you can imagine. For what purpose? And prompted by what agenda?

We'll get to that.

It's surprising then that on the same website we find an article from 2014 that spells out how frequently America has been involved in coups around the world that have destroyed democracy in at least 30 countries, while here at home, we are told that we live in a democracy that is the envy of the world.

What we are not told, and what our research discovers, is that democracy in America is a lie - a cover - and a front for a subtle, almost silent coup which requires either the co-operation of President Trump, or his removal from office if he fails to go along to get along.

Certainly it may be hoped that his "America First" campaign rhetoric will prove to be his true intent, but the record shows that previous presidents with similar intentions suddenly found themselves terminated with extreme prejudice - or by "wet work" as it is called in some circles.

Others were either hand picked for the office by the "controllers," or were blackmailed into joining their camp once they were inaugurated.

While there are millions of sincere Democrats in America who want the very best for their country, and millions of their counterparts among the Republicans, those millions who believe in the sanctity and the role of the two-party system have no clue that America is really controlled by a shadow government, the "Deep State" the Globalists (call them by whatever name, they have the same goal).

So because of the corruption and control these people have within politics, especially at the federal level, they have, over a period of decades, morphed national politics into what is now a one-agenda system that has two heads - Democrats and Republicans. It doesn't matter who is in power - the agenda is always being pushed forward by adherents in both parties.

The goal of this hydra-headed bottom-dweller has always been world control, but standing in their way was this confounded country of free-thinkers who had established a Republic - a new form of self-governance that the founders believed would avoid the rise of tyranny and dictatorship, both of which are synonymous with democracy, as history has shown time and again.

How did this fixation on democracy in America, as opposed to being a true republic, come about? By deliberate intent.

And the Federal (Not) Reserve Bank, controlled by those private interests we have referred to elsewhere - in particular those within the Rothschild cartel - made it happen, not just with the election of President Wilson in 1913, but through what in hindsight appears to have been a massive subterfuge in the 1930s.

The version of those events for public consumption, written by Robert Jabaily of the Federal Reserve Bank of Boston, is that the Federal Reserve ran into trouble in the 1930s because it didn't have enough gold to back the currency that was in circulation.

His article is a version of the truth that reads well, suggesting that the Great Depression and the associated Bank Holiday all came about by accident, with no mention of the fact that the banks which claimed to be on the verge of insolvency were doing so deliberately, in order to create chaos across America, leading to a solution which would increase their control of both the government, and the people of America.

To quote briefly from Jabaily's article:- *"At 1:00 a.m. on Monday, March 6, (1933) President Roosevelt issued Proclamation 2039 ordering the suspension of all banking transactions, effective immediately. He had taken the oath of office only thirty-six hours earlier. For an entire week, Americans would have no access to banks or banking services. They could not withdraw or transfer their money, nor could they make deposits."*

Believe the official version, written by the Federal Reserve itself, if you wish. Or see the situation as but one of many moves on a Rothschild chess board on which even Presidents are seen as pawns (often willing ones) in a game that will eventually see the true controllers prevail. Or at least that's the plan.

Having absolutely no allegiance to any country or any political system, the Globalists were and are determined to wipe out all competition. Therefore it is no surprise to learn that thousands of smaller banks went belly up - thanks to recommendations by the Federal Reserve - thus consolidating more power within the banks that remained.

Better yet - for the banks - "Treasury Secretary William Woodin ... decided to ... "issue currency against the sound assets of the banks [as opposed to issuing currency against gold]. The Federal Reserve Act lets us print all we'll need. And it won't frighten the people. It won't look like stage money. It'll be money that looks like real money." - Federal Reserve Bank of Boston 1999.

Yes folks, what looks like "real money" has enabled the Government to print all it needs, and generate today's debt of $20 trillion and rising - by the minute.

Looking at that debt, it would seem to be obvious that through their Bank Holiday strategy the Globalists managed to use their control over money, with the assistance of their friendly politicians, to bring America, and many of its people, to the point of bankruptcy.

But for them, that was not enough. After all, their aim has always been world control, under a One World Government within a New World Order. And you can't achieve that if any one country insists on being a Republic. The Republic would have to be destroyed.

But how could you do that?

Change The Nation

To do that, you would have to change the consciousness of an entire nation, a feat which might take several generations, but once achieved you are well on the way to the coup d'etat, the fulfillment of that silent coup you have planned for so long.

For them, including the UnAmerican Americans among them, it was essential to wipe from people's memory any understanding of the difference between a democracy and a republic; change their brains in such a way that "democracy" would be seen by future generations as synonymous with the intentions of the Founding Fathers, the essence of The Constitution, and even as the envy of countries around the world.

The truth is, a republic is 180 degrees different from a democracy. And a democracy is the opposite of what the Founding Fathers and those who died for the republic had in mind. A democracy, which we are currently told to believe is America's birthright, and the envy of the world, to fight and die for, has been shown throughout history to result in discontent and anarchy - and worse.

It was the failings of a democracy that brought Hitler to Power in the 1930s.

From 1928 into the 1930s the US military in particular had its own very clear definitions of the difference between a democracy and a republic, which America still was, at that time. Those differences were clearly spelled out, and could be used in any court of law, if required. Yet, strangely, those clear definitions would disappear, under orders from the White House - and future generations would have no clue what the difference between a democracy and a republic really is.

Democracy v Republic

The US War Department, under the aegis of the then Chief of Staff of the United States Army, issued a 156 page book on November 30, 1928, in which the differences between a democracy and a republic were clearly defined.

Democracy:"A government of the masses. Authority derived through mass meeting or any other form of "direct" expression. Results in mobocracy. Attitude toward property is communistic - negating property rights. Attitude toward law is that the will of the majority shall regulate, whether is be based upon deliberation or governed by passion, prejudice, and impulse, without restraint or regard to consequences. Results in demogogism, license, agitation, discontent, anarchy."

Republic:"Authority is derived through the election by the people of public officials best fitted to represent them. Attitude toward law is the administration of justice in accord with fixed principles and established evidence, with a strict regard to consequences. A greater number of citizens and extent of territory may be brought within its compass. Avoids the dangerous extreme of either tyranny or mobocracy. Results in statesmanship, liberty, reason, justice, contentment, and progress. Is the "standard form" of government throughout the world. A republic is a form of government under a constitution which provides for the election of

(1) an executive and (2) a legislative body, who working together in a representative capacity, have all the power of appointment, all power of legislation, all power to raise revenue and appropriate expenditures, and are required to create (3) a judiciary to pass upon the justice and legality of their government acts and to recognize (4) certain inherent individual rights.

"By order of the Secretary of War: C.P. Summerall, Major General, Chief of Staff. Official: Lutz Wahl, Major General, The Adjutant General.

Shortly after the "bank holiday" in the thirties, hush-hush orders from the White House suddenly demanded that all copies of this book be withdrawn from the Government Printing Office and the Army posts, to be suppressed and destroyed without explanation.

History has shown that a democracy cannot exist as a permanent form of Government.

"It can only exist until the voters discover they can vote themselves largess out of the public treasury.

"From that moment on the majority always votes for the candidate promising the most benefits from the public treasury with the result that Democracy always collapses over a loose fiscal policy, always to be followed by a Dictatorship." [Written by Professor Alexander Fraser Tytler, nearly two centuries ago while our thirteen original states were still colonies of Great Britain. At the time he was writing of the decline and fall of the Athenian Republic over two thousand years before.]

What Reagan Said

"This idea that government was beholden to the people, that it had no other source of power is still the newest, most unique idea in all the long history of man's relation to man. This is the issue of this election: Whether we believe in our capacity for self-government or whether we abandon the American Revolution and confess that a little intellectual elite in a far-distant capital can plan our lives for us better than we can plan them ourselves." - Ronald Reagan's Speech at the 1964 National Convention: *"A Time for Choosing."*

Remember, President Reagan, who spoke of "an intellectual elite in a far distant capital" survived an assassination attempt. Others haven't.

Donald Trump said something very similar in his inauguration speech, "For too long, a small group in our nation's capital has reaped the rewards of government while the people have borne the cost."

But what is the cost of being a president? Knowing that others before you have been assassinated, how fearless would you have to be to stand up to that "small group," which in reality has a vast reach.

Unless this new president can pull something out of the bag, a rabbit out of the hat, or a few snakes out of the swamp, what future America? A democracy gone mad? A "summer of rage" that will play into the hands of the coup plotters? A gift for the Globalists? Because that's what they're after with this silent coup that has been underway, not just in the past few weeks and months against Donald Trump, but for generations against the people of America and the Republic itself.

If there is any good news to relate, it is that there are indeed more than a few people awake to what is going on.

Both President Reagan and President Trump have shown their awareness in their speeches, and other presidents have also openly declared that there is a secret power at work.

The memorial to President Franklin Delano Roosevelt bears the following epitaph:- *"They who seek to establish systems of government based on the regimentation of all human beings by a handful of individual rulers call this a new order. It is not new and it is not order."*

President Roosevelt was the man who aided the banks in their quest to take America off the gold standard, and whose White House removed that Army manual and its definitions of a democracy and a republic from circulation. We may never know for sure, but perhaps he, like others before and since, was blackmailed or threatened in order to make him go along with that secret power that has bedeviled America ever since its founding.

It is the UnAmerican Americans and their friends among the banks and the Globalists, the sycophants in the mainstream media, their trolls on the Internet, the empty talking heads on television, who are the enemy within.

They rely on our complacency, our ignorance about the difference between a democracy and a republic, knowing that democracies always destroy themselves, and those who are left will be more than happy to embrace the New World Order. Then they will call the coup complete.

Good Luck With That....

Last Word - A New Time

If President Trump is as fearless as Ramtha says he is, and if things pan out in the way Ramtha has said they will, then the future will be a lot brighter than these dark headlines would have us expect.

If he is to "know it all" as Ramtha has said, one thing he will know, if he doesn't already, is that among the elite, there are hundreds, and probably thousands of pedophiles, child abusers, and sex traffickers; perverts in places of high office who have protected each other for many years.

As unpleasant as it is to raise the matter, this is not a conspiracy theory. As in the days of Sodom and Gomorrah, among those who purport to be the leaders of the world there are depraved people. Not that this is a new phenomenon. It has been going on for thousands of years, its practitioners hiding behind religion, or hiding behind their positions of power.

It happens in Hollywood. It happens in Washington DC. It happens in Britain and other countries in Europe. It happens throughout the world.

In February, the Free Thought Project reported on the fact that in Britain, the police chief came forward and confirmed that the former Prime Minister of England, Sir Edward Heath, had raped dozens of children. The department also noted how those within the government helped cover up these crimes.

That is the sort of swamp that President Trump has to deal with. Not until it is finally drained can we expect to see the changes that Ramtha forecast long ago.

If he survives the mainstream media attacks and the leaks and nasty innuendo from his adversaries who are supporters of the Deep State, President Trump is set to be in office for at least four years.

If, as Ramtha says, a couple of UFOs already have or are going to appear alongside President Trump's plane and wave at him, and subsequently he will "know it all" then we might assume that while The Donald has many enemies in low places, he also has good friends in high places.

While "hope" became a hollow word after the election of the last president, perhaps it is time to resurrect that word in regards to the future.

One thing is certain. It will be a future of ongoing and final efforts by the Illuminati to impose their One World Order amid ongoing Earth Changes which Ramtha has long warned will include great natural disasters.

Nevertheless, the future is not all bad - not bad at all - eventually.

Ramtha:- *"In this civilization you have great truth coming your way, an opportunity, and this civilization will not collapse. The meek will inherit the Earth and see the glory of God, for they will have the eyes to see it.*

"Know the truth. Be enlightened, engaged, and knowing. Superconsciousness, which is yet to be dreamed and experienced, is worth hanging around and seeing for yourself. - Ramtha, *"Last Waltz Of The Tyrants,"* pp 136/137.

"I can tell you something of nature in its violent actions and its movement to destroy the possibilities of this goal for a one world government. When the food gets short and the people are in revolt, all those people who have held their tongue for so long are going

to start screaming, are going to tell it all, are going to point fingers, and the truth will be let out to the whole world. Superconsciousness will come even in that, and if their plan succeeds and the vacuum collapses, you will see an armada perhaps like you only thought existed in fairy tales and superstition. They do exist." - Ramtha, *"Last Waltz of the Tyrants,"* p 132.

Ramtha - People Will Rise Up

"The radical nation in the last days is this country, this land, the nation of a radical people that will rise up against its enslaver, and its greatest message is coming from the North." - Ramtha, *"Last Waltz of the Tyrants,"* p 91.

Suggested Books

The Tower of Basel - http://amzn.to/2tuuZZ9

The *Unseen Hand* - http://amzn.to/2g4RUYF

Other Books by Ramtha

Last Waltz Of The Tyrants - http://amzn.to/2bbPtxg

UFOs And The Nature of Reality - http://amzn.to/1GPMaFx

The White Book - Hard Cover - http://amzn.to/2bC96xV

The White Book - Kindle Edition - http://amzn.to/2bqvoED

by JZ Knight

A State of Mind - http://amzn.to/2blwDWp

Suggested Websites

These are not endorsements - just suggestions for your further personal research.

President Trump's Accomplishments During His First 6 Months: http://allthiswinning.com/index

For articles both for and against Trump - www.alternet.org and http://www.breitbart.com/

Review Request

Your voluntary review of this book on Amazon would be much appreciated.

As a customer you can simply go online to Amazon, do a search under Books for *"President Trump And The New World Order,"* select this book, then do a review in your own words.

Made in the USA
Middletown, DE
02 January 2022

57451667R00070